CLASSICS ONE STEP AT A TIME

THE ULTIMATE STEP-BY-STEP COOKBOOK

KEDA BLACK

PHOTOGRAPHY FRÉDÉRIC LUCANO • STYLING SONIA LUCANO

❋ ❋ ❋

hamlyn

First published in France in 2007 under the title *Les Basiques*, by Hachette Livre (Marabout)

Photography by Frédéric Lucano
Styling by Sonia Lucano

An Hachette UK Company
www.hachette.co.uk

First published in Great Britain in 2009 by
Hamlyn, a division of Octopus Publishing Group Ltd
2–4 Heron Quays, London E14 4JP
www.octopusbooks.co.uk

ISBN 978-0-600-61952-9

A CIP catalogue record for this book is available from the British Library

Printed and bound in Singapore

10 9 8 7 6 5 4 3 2 1

Measurements Metric and imperial measurements have been given in all recipes. Use one set of measurements only and not a mixture of both. Standard level spoon measurements are used in all recipes.
1 tablespoon = one 15 ml spoon
1 teaspoon = one 5 ml spoon

Nuts This book includes dishes made with nuts and nut derivatives. It is advisable for those with known allergic reactions to nuts and nut derivatives and those who may be potentially vulnerable to these allergies, such as pregnant and nursing mothers, invalids, the elderly, babies and children, to avoid dishes made with nuts and nut oils. It is also advisable to check the labels of preprepared ingredients for the possible inclusion of nut derivatives.

Eggs should be large unless otherwise stated. The Department of Health advises that eggs should not be consumed raw. This book contains dishes made with raw or lightly cooked eggs. It is advisable for more vulnerable people, such as pregnant and nursing mothers, invalids, the elderly, babies and young children, to avoid uncooked or lightly cooked dishes made with eggs. Once prepared these dishes should be kept refrigerated and used promptly.

Milk should be full fat unless otherwise stated.

Butter is unsalted unless otherwise stated.

Fresh herbs should be used unless otherwise stated. If unavailable use dried herbs as an alternative but halve the quantities stated.

Ovens should be preheated to the specific temperature – if using a fan-assisted oven, follow manufacturer's instructions for adjusting the time and the temperature.

FOREWORD

This book is a collection of indispensable recipes: the basics that never go out of fashion, with a modern twist (steak and chips, roast chicken, pumpkin soup, pan-fried scallops, floating islands…), and new classics, just wonderful as they are (rabbit tagine, light moussaka, pasta with pesto, courgette crumble, cheesecake…). Here are 80 recipes that you should master once and for all!

To ensure not a single one is ever a failure, the method is foolproof: for each crucial stage in a recipe there is a photograph. The mysteries of Béarnaise sauce, shown step by step, become clear. Every stage for preparing beef braised in beer or wine is illustrated; it's as easy as ABC. See in full colour how to make real mayonnaise; how to whiz up a gazpacho in the blender; or how to incorporate flour with egg before it is blended with milk to become perfect pancake batter that spreads in the frying pan until it can be flipped over and devoured with jam. Delicious!

And there you have it! For the beginner cook, the essentials; for the weekend cook, more culinary know-how; and, for the advanced, great new ideas. All with photographs and every one of them simplicity itself!

CONTENTS

THE CLASSICS

1

2

3

4

5

6

1	Put the egg yolks in a large mixing bowl.	2	Add the salt and mustard.	3	Beat with a hand-held electric whisk.
4	Pour in a drop of oil and beat. Continue adding oil a drop at a time and beat until the mixture thickens.	5	After a third of the oil is added, pour in a steady thin stream, while beating continuously.	6	Once the mayonnaise has become really thick, season with a little lemon juice and pepper.

02

CLASSIC VINAIGRETTE

SERVES 4 • PREPARATION: 5 MINUTES

1 tablespoon red wine vinegar
⅛ teaspoon salt
½–1 teaspoon French mustard
3 tablespoons olive oil
a few grindings of pepper

SALADS

BASICS

EGGS

STEAK & CO.

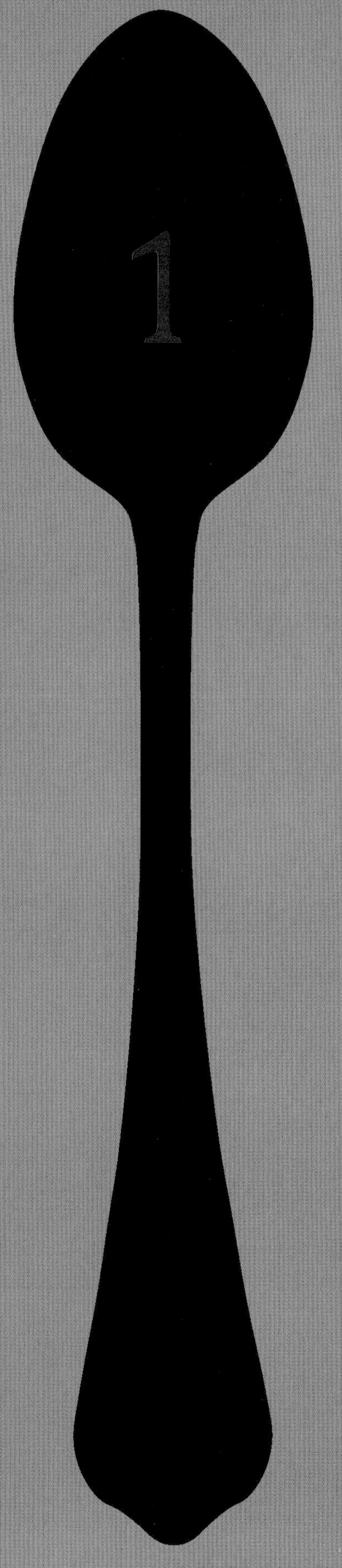

01

MAYONNAISE

MAKES 300 ML (10 FL OZ) • PREPARATION: 15 MINUTES

2 egg yolks
½ teaspoon salt
½ teaspoon Dijon mustard (optional)

300 ml (10 fl oz) oil (one part sunflower to two parts olive oil)
½–1 teaspoon lemon juice
freshly ground pepper

FOR AÏOLI (GARLIC MAYONNAISE):
Crush 2–5 garlic cloves with the salt in a small bowl before adding in the egg yolks.

1

2

3

4

5

6

1	Mix the vinegar with the salt then add the mustard.	2	Add the oil, a little at a time, while stirring.	3	Season with pepper.
			OPTION SHAKER		
4	Put everything into a clean jam jar.	5	Screw on the lid tightly and shake the jar.	6	It's ready to serve.

03

GARLIC VINAIGRETTE

VARIATION ON CLASSIC VINAIGRETTE

- 1 small garlic clove
- ⅛ teaspoon salt
- 1 tablespoon lemon juice
- 3 tablespoons olive oil
- freshly ground pepper

Crush the peeled garlic with the salt using a pestle and mortar or a small spoon until it forms a paste.

Add the lemon juice, mix well, then stir in the oil and lightly season with pepper.

ALL LEMON VINAIGRETTE

VARIATION ON CLASSIC VINAIGRETTE

1 tablespoon lemon juice
3 tablespoons olive oil
⅛ teaspoon salt
rind of ½ lemon

☛ Mix everything together!

05

VERY GREEN SALAD

SERVES 4 • PREPARATION: 15 MINUTES

1 lettuce of your choice: green oak leaf, romaine, curly leaf lettuce, frisée, etc
Vinaigrette (see recipe 02)
½ bunch of chives, chopped
leaves from 4 chervil stalks, chopped
leaves from 4 tarragon stalks, chopped
fronds from 4 dill stalks, chopped
leaves from 4 mints stalks, chopped
3–4 spring onions, green parts included (optional), chopped

CUSTOMIZE YOUR VINAIGRETTE:
You can add, for example, a little crème fraiche for romaine, some crushed blue cheese for frisée, walnut oil for escarole...

1	Remove the base of the lettuce and discard any outer leaves that have spoiled. Separate the good leaves and plunge into cold water.	2	Drain and repeat in clean water. Do not allow the leaves to remain soaking in the water. Dry them well, preferably in a salad spinner.
3	Tear up any large leaves and put them all in a large salad bowl.	4	Drizzle over the vinaigrette and stir to coat the leaves. Add the chopped herbs and spring onions. Stir again and serve.

06

BÉCHAMEL SAUCE

MAKES 600 ML (1 PINT) • PREPARATION: 2 MINUTES • COOKING: 15 MINUTES

50 g (2 oz) butter
40 g (1½ oz) flour
600 ml (1 pint) milk
salt and freshly ground pepper
pinch of freshly grated nutmeg
1 knob of butter or 1 tablespoon crème fraîche (optional)

1	Gently melt the butter in a small saucepan over a medium heat.	2	Remove from the heat and tip in the flour in one go.	3	Mix with a wooden spoon.
4	Return the pan to the heat and add the milk little by little (1 tablespoon then 2 tablespoons at a time).	5	Incorporate all the milk then allow the sauce to cook for 7–8 minutes over a very gentle heat.	6	Season with the salt, pepper and nutmeg. For a richer sauce, stir in the butter or crème fraîche.

07

CHEESE SOUFFLÉ

SERVES 2 • PREPARATION: 15 MINUTES • COOKING: 35 MINUTES

butter, for greasing
300 ml (½ pint) Béchamel Sauce (see recipe 06), prepared and cooled
75 g (3 oz) grated cheese (Emmental, Cheddar or another hard variety)
pinch of cayenne pepper
pinch of caraway or cumin seeds, crushed (optional)
3 eggs

IN ADVANCE:
Butter a 1-litre (1¾ pint) soufflé dish. Preheat the oven to 190°C (375°F), Gas Mark 5.

1 2
3 4

1	Incorporate the grated cheese and the spices into the just-cooled bechamel sauce.	2	Separate the eggs.	
3	Beat the egg yolks and stir into the sauce.	4	Whisk the egg whites until they form firm peaks.	➢

07

5	Beat in 2 tablespoons of egg white into the sauce. Fold in the remaining whites very delicately, lifting the mixture as you go, using a metal tablespoon or slotted spoon.	**GOOD TO KNOW** ☛ A slotted spoon is a really useful tool for folding whisked egg whites into a mixture (savoury or sweet). It allows you to cut through the mixture without losing all the air.

6	Carefully pour the mixture into the prepared dish and transfer to the oven. Cook for 35 minutes. Serve at once, with green salad.

TIP

For a well-risen soufflé, don't be tempted to open the oven door while it is cooking!

TIP

You can reserve a little of the grated cheese to sprinkle over the surface. It forms a light crust which helps the soufflé underneath to rise.

VARIATIONS

Of course, you can try different cheese varieties: a blue, Double Gloucester…

08

SHORTCRUST PASTRY

FOR A 23-CM (9-INCH) TART TO SERVE 4 • PREPARATION: 15 MINUTES • RESTING: 1 HOUR MINIMUM

250 g (8 oz) flour
½ teaspoon salt

125 g (4 oz) butter (if you use salted butter, omit the salt)
cold water to mix

PREPARE AHEAD:
Shortcrust pastry can be made up to 2 days in advance of use. It also freezes very well.

1 2 3

4 5 6

1	Put the flour, the salt and the butter, cut into cubes, in a large bowl.	2	Use your fingertips to rub the butter into the flour until it resembles breadcrumbs.	3	Add half a glass of cold water and mix in using a round-bladed knife.
4	The dough will combine.	5	Finish forming the dough into a ball by lightly working with your hands. On no account work it heavily.	6	Put the dough into a plastic bag or wrap in cling film and place in the fridge to rest for at least 1 hour.

09

QUICHE LORRAINE

SERVES 4 • PREPARATION: 15 MINUTES • COOKING: 50 MINUTES

butter, for greasing
150 g (5 oz) smoked bacon
Shortcrust Pastry (see recipe 08)
3 large eggs

300 ml (½ pint) whipping cream (full- or half-fat)
pinch of freshly grated nutmeg
salt and pepper

IN ADVANCE:
Grease a 23-cm (9-inch) quiche tin. Preheat the oven to 180°C (350°F), Gas Mark 4. Cut the bacon into small dice.

1	Brown off the bacon in a frying pan.	2	Roll out the pastry and use to line the quiche tin. Prick the base with a fork then place the tin in the fridge.	3	Put the cooked bacon in the pastry-lined tin.
4	Mix the eggs with the cream and the nutmeg. Add a little salt and pepper.	5	Pour the cream mixture into the quiche tin.	6	Transfer to the oven for 35–40 minutes until the top is golden-brown.

FRESH PIZZA MARGARITA

SERVES 2 • PREPARATION: 10 MINUTES • COOKING: 15 MINUTES

500 g (1 lb) prepared bread dough from a quality baker or a ready-made pizza base
250 ml (8 fl oz) Tomato Sauce (see recipe 20)

250 g (8 oz) mozzarella, preferably made with buffalo milk
leaves from 4 basil stalks

IN ADVANCE:
Preheat the oven to its highest setting. Keep the bread dough in the fridge until 1 hour before you want to make the pizza.

1	Roll out the dough on a lightly floured pastry board. If it springs back too much, leave it to rest a little before rolling out further.	2	Place the dough on a baking sheet and spread with tomato sauce.
3	Tear the mozzarella into small pieces with your fingers and scatter evenly over the pizza.	4	Transfer the pizza to the oven and cook for 10–15 minutes, depending on the thickness of the base. Garnish with torn basil leaves and serve.

BOILED EGG & SPICE BREAD

SERVES 1 • PREPARATION: 5 MINUTES • COOKING: 10 MINUTES

1 egg
butter
bread and spice bread to make fingers
salt

VARIATION:
Very classy: try shavings of dried salted fish roe (sold as poutargue or bottarga) with this simple meal.

You can also use breadsticks for dipping into the egg.

1 2
3 4

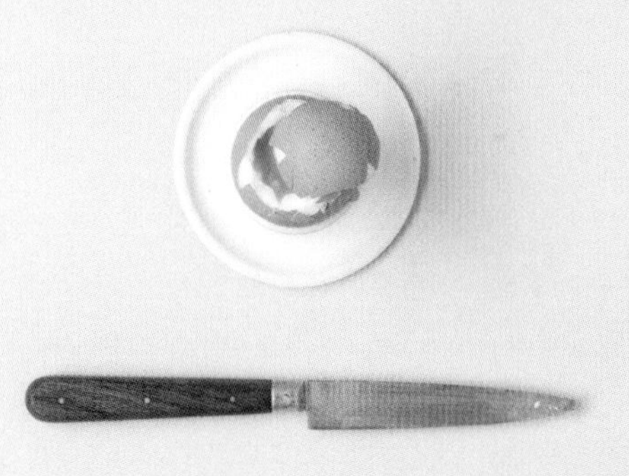

1	Place the egg in a small saucepan and cover with cold water.	2	Bring to the boil then cook for 3 minutes.
3	Drain and immediately open the top with a small sharp knife.	4	Serve the boiled egg with buttered fingers of bread and spice bread and a little salt.

12

SOFT BOILED EGG & ASPARAGUS

SERVES 1 • PREPARATION: 5 MINUTES • COOKING: 13 MINUTES

1 egg
asparagus stalks, cooked
olive oil
sea salt flakes

OTHER IDEAS:
This is also delicious with a rocket or dandelion salad, with bacon, or as part of a salade niçoise.

1 2

3 4

1	Place the egg in a small pan covered with cold water.	2	Bring to the boil and cook for 6 minutes.
3	Plunge the egg into cold water, then shell.	4	Serve on a bed of asparagus stalks, with a drizzle of olive oil and the salt flakes.

13

CORSICAN OMELETTE

SERVES 1 • PREPARATION: 5 MINUTES • COOKING: 5 MINUTES

3 eggs
salt and freshly ground pepper
15 g (½ oz) butter

2 tablespoons drained ricotta, fromage frais or cottage cheese
leaves from 2 mint stalks

OTHER IDEAS:
Use different cheese and herbs of your choosing.

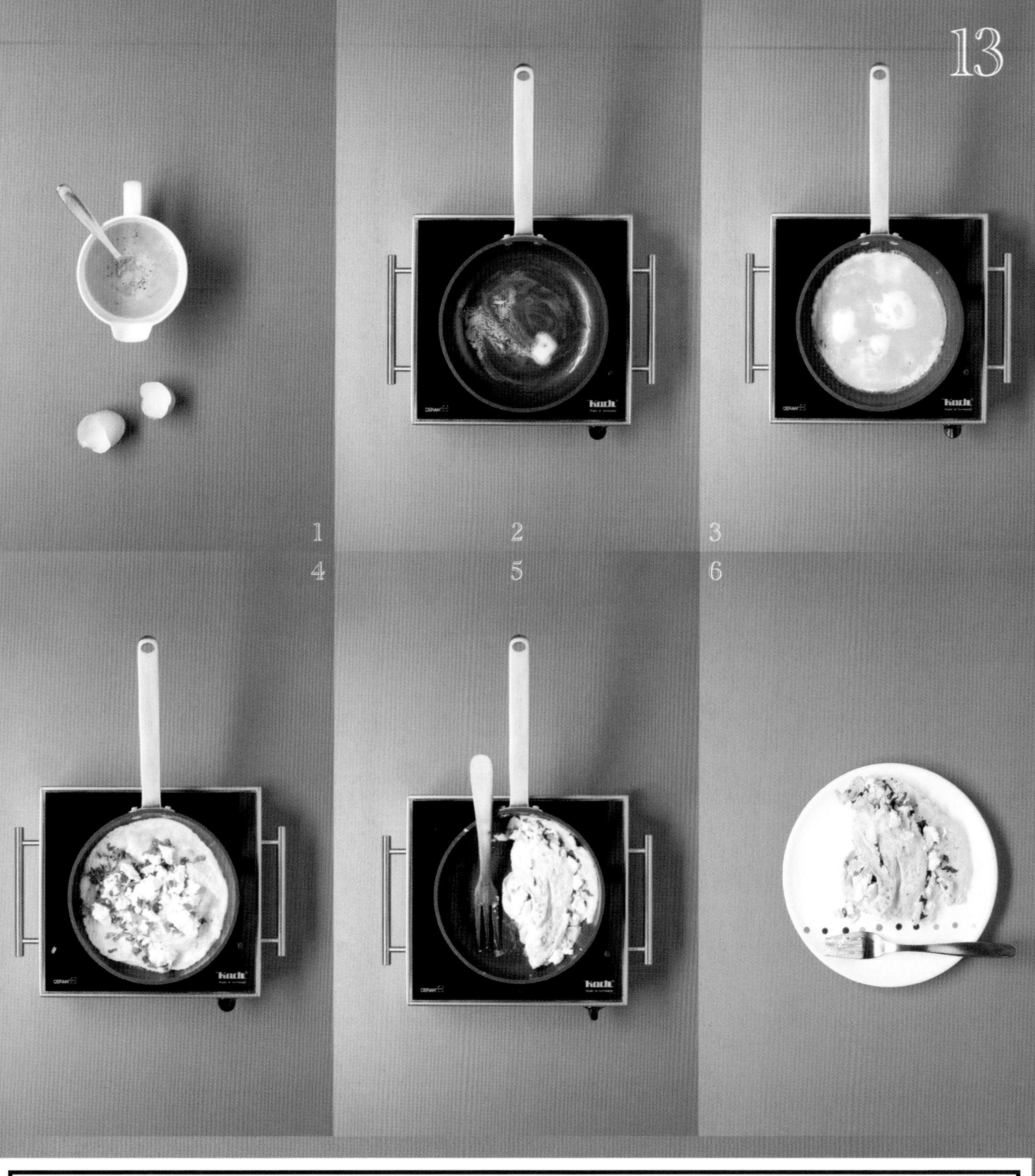

1	Crack the eggs, break the yolks with a fork then season to taste with salt and pepper.	2	Melt the butter in a small frying pan over a medium-high heat. When it foams, add the beaten eggs.	3	When the base of the omelette is set, tilt the pan so that the uncooked egg runs to the sides of the hot pan.
4	Sprinkle the cheese and torn mint leaves over the omelette.	5	Fold the omelette in half, turn off the heat and leave to cook for 2–4 minutes.	6	Slide out onto a plate.

14

SCRAMBLED EGGS

SERVES 1 • PREPARATION: 5 MINUTES • COOKING: 10 MINUTES

20 g (¾ oz) butter
4 eggs
salt and freshly ground pepper
½ bunch of chervil and ½ bunch of chives, chopped

OTHER IDEAS:
Garnish your scrambled eggs with smoked salmon (or with truffle shavings for the deluxe version), or with Tabasco sauce and coriander for a Mexican-style brunch.

14

1	Melt the butter in a small frying pan over a gentle heat.	2	Crack the eggs into a bowl, mix without beating then season with salt and pepper.
3	Tip the eggs into the pan and cook, stirring continuously with a wooden spoon, until they are set to a creamy consistency.	4	Add the chopped herbs and serve.

15

CLASSIC STEAK

SERVES 2 • PREPARATION: 2 MINUTES • COOKING: 4 MINUTES

2 beef steaks about 1 cm (½ in) thick, each weighing 200 g (7 oz)
1 tablespoon olive oil
salt and freshly ground pepper

IN ADVANCE:
Lightly oil the steaks then pepper them.

IS IT COOKED?
The steak is cooked rare when it yields slightly to the pressure of a finger – or cut it to see if the inside is done to your liking.

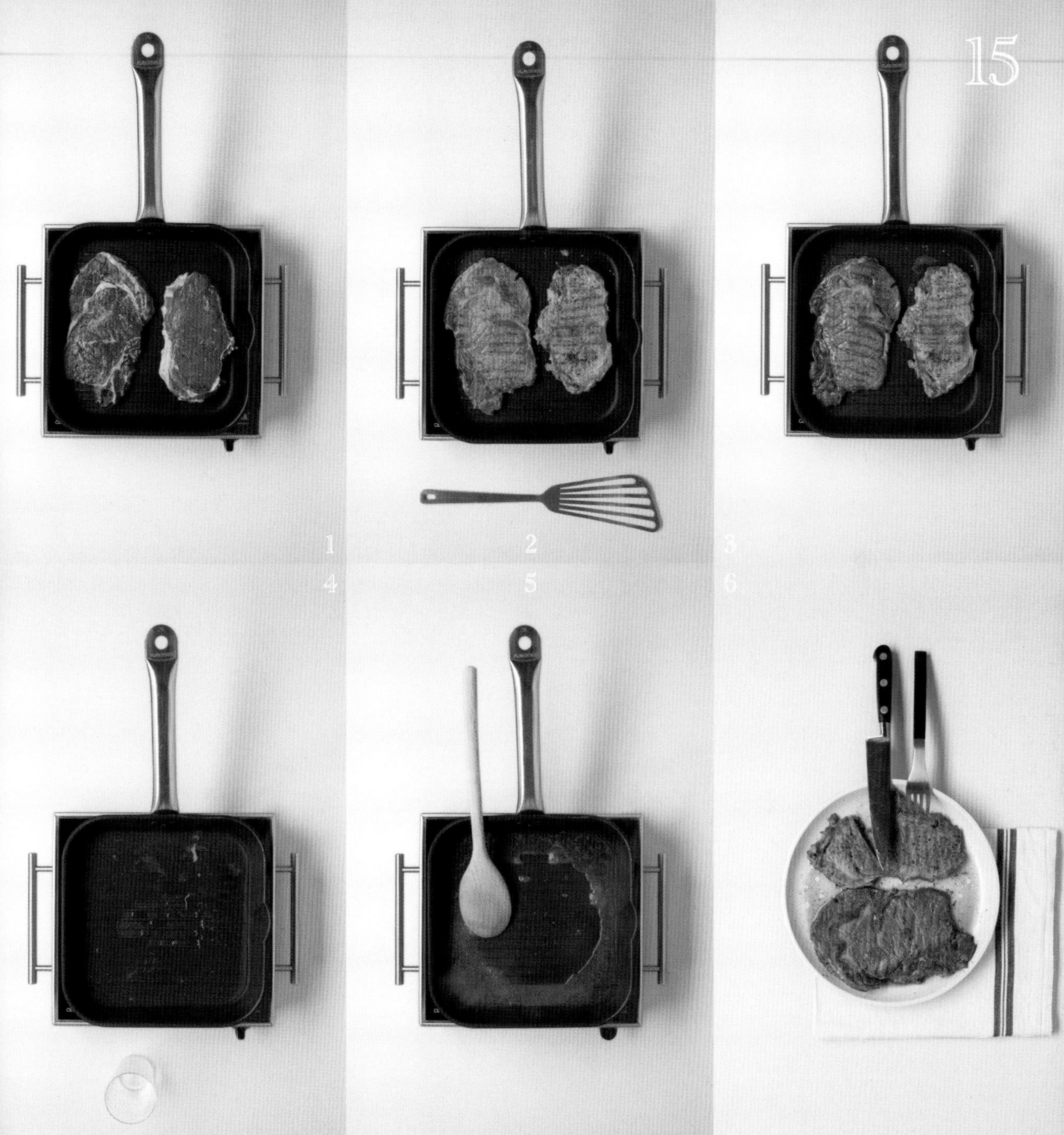

1	Preheat a heavy-based frying pan. Put in the steaks, press with a spatula and cook for 2 minutes.	2	Turn over the steaks, season with salt and cook again for 2 minutes, pressing down with a spatula.	3	Test the steaks are done to your liking (see the tip). Put the steak on warm serving plates.
4	Return the pan to the heat and pour in half a glass of water.	5	Scrape up any caramelized bits and let the water boil and evaporate a little.	6	Pour these cooking juices over the steaks and serve.

16

BÉARNAISE SAUCE

SERVES 2 • PREPARATION: 5 MINUTES • COOKING: 10 MINUTES

2 small shallots
50 ml (2 fl oz) tarragon vinegar or white wine
4 peppercorns
3 tarragon stalks

2 egg yolks
150 g (5 oz) soft butter, cut into cubes
salt

IN ADVANCE:
Peel and finely chop the shallots.

1	Put the shallots into a small saucepan with the vinegar, peppercorns and tarragon.	2	Bring to the boil, allow to reduce, then remove the peppercorns and herbs.	3	Put the egg yolks in a small bowl over a pan of gently simmering water.
4	Add the reduced vinegar and whisk to combine.	5	Whisk in the butter, a cube at a time. Turn off the heat once half the butter has been added.	6	Continue to add the butter off the heat. The sauce should become rich and thick. Season with salt.

17

BLUE CHEESE SAUCE

SERVES 2 • PREPARATION: 2 MINUTES • COOKING: 5 MINUTES

100 g (3½ oz) blue cheese
200 ml (7 fl oz) crème fraîche
(not the reduced-fat version)
freshly ground pepper

1 2

3 4

1	Put the cheese with 1 or 2 spoonfuls of the crème fraîche in a small pan.	2	Allow to melt over a gentle heat.
3	Add the remaining crème fraîche and bring to the boil, stirring all the time with a wooden spoon.	4	Remove from the heat when the sauce is thick enough to coat the back of the spoon. Season with pepper.

GREEN PEPPERCORN SAUCE

SERVES 2 • PREPARATION: 2 MINUTES • COOKING: 10 MINUTES

100 ml (3½ fl oz) white wine vinegar
1 shallot
1–1½ teaspoons green peppercorns in brine, drained
200 ml (7 fl oz) crème fraîche
1 teaspoon Dijon mustard
salt (optional)

18

1	Put the vinegar in a small saucepan with a small glass of water. Gently bring to the boil.	2	Chop the shallot finely and add to the boiling vinegar. Allow to cook for a few minutes until the liquid is reduced to 2 tablespoons. Remove from the heat.
3	Discard the shallot. Add the peppercorns to the reduction. Return the pan to the heat and add the crème fraîche and the mustard.	4	Bring to the boil. Allow the sauce to further reduce on a very gentle heat for 2–3 minutes. Taste and season with salt if necessary.

19

CHIPS

SERVES 2 • PREPARATION: 15 MINUTES • COOKING: 10 MINUTES

4 large floury potatoes suitable for making chips or mash
2 litres (3½ pints) vegetable oil
salt, to serve

USING A DEEP FRYER:
Remove the basket from the fryer.
Pour in the oil and switch on the fryer.
Preheat the fryer to 150°C (300°).

TEST:
Drop one chip into the oil. If it is hot enough, the chip should rise to the surface and create small bubbles.

1

2

3

4

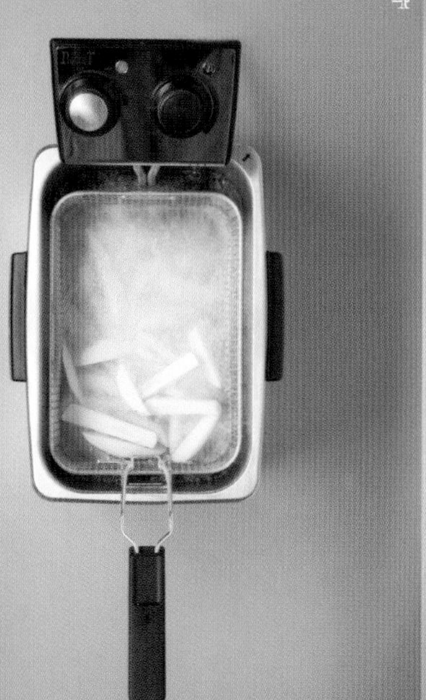

5

6

1	Peel the potatoes.	2	Cut them into chips about 1 cm (½ in) thick.	3	Put the chips into a large bowl of cold water to stop them turning brown.
4	Drain and dry the chips on kitchen paper. Place them in the basket and lower carefully into the hot oil.	5	Deep-fry for 5 minutes. Do not overload the fryer; it's better to cook this stage in batches if necessary.	6	Fry all the chips for another 3–4 minutes until golden. Drain on kitchen paper, sprinkle with salt and serve.

PASTA & RICE

SAUCES

PASTA

RICE

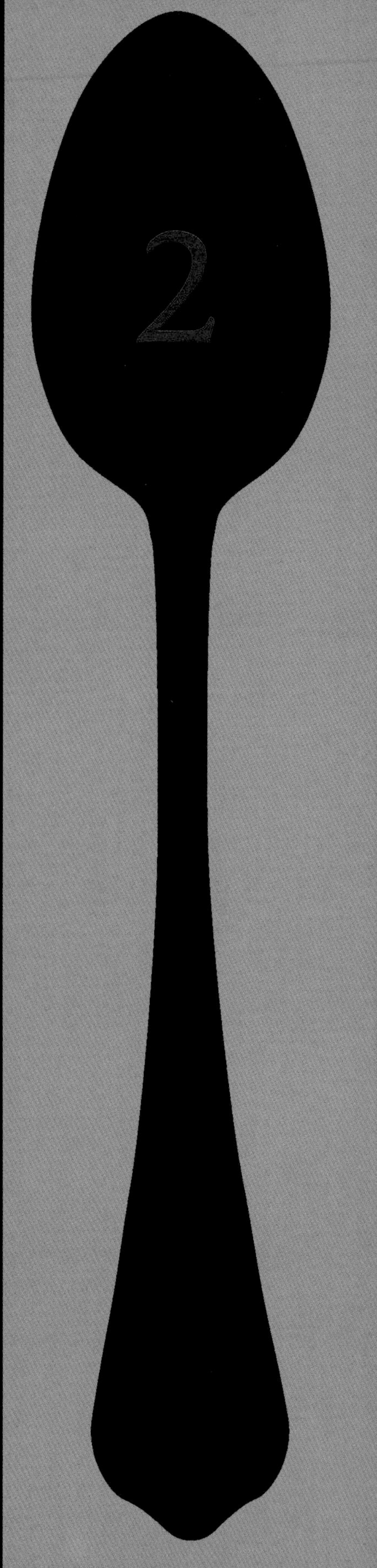

CHERRY TOMATO SAUCE

SERVES 2 • PREPARATION: 5 MINUTES • COOKING: 25 MINUTES

1 tablespoon olive oil
1 onion, chopped
1 garlic clove, peeled, crushed and finely chopped
500 g (1 lb) cherry tomatoes
2 thyme sprigs and/or 4 basil stalks
salt and freshly ground pepper
½ teaspoon sugar (optional)
½ teaspoon butter (optional)

Using cherry tomatoes gives a sauce with more texture (and often more flavour) but of course you can also substitute ordinary tomatoes.

1 Heat the oil in a frying pan over a medium heat. Soften the onion and garlic for 5 minutes, without colouring.

OPTIONAL SPICE

Sprinkle the onion and garlic with a teaspoonful of curry spices or the North African mix, ras-el-hanout, for a sauce that is very good with egg dishes.

TO MAKE PIPERADE

Add 1 or 2 finely chopped red peppers to the onion and garlic as they soften in the frying pan. At the end of cooking, add 2 eggs and stir gently as if making scrambled eggs. The result is similar to piperade, a classic dish from southwest France, which is a cross between an omelette and scrambled eggs.

➢

2	Add the tomatoes, the thyme and/or basil leaves and salt and pepper. Mix well then allow to cook, uncovered, for 20 minutes over a low-medium heat.

NOTE

A little sugar helps the flavour of tomatoes if they haven't had enough sun to ripen fully.

TIP

☛ If you are using ordinary tomatoes it is best to skin them first. Plunge them in boiling water for 1 minute then the skins slip off easily.

3	At the end of cooking the sauce should be well reduced. Taste, adjust the seasoning and add a little sugar if necessary.

NOTE

Adding a little butter to the sauce makes it richer.

OTHER IDEAS

Stir the sauce if you want it to be smooth. This sauce is good for pasta and as a pizza topping. It is delicious served with grilled sliced aubergine. Add 150 ml (¼ pint) coconut milk and a pinch of saffron threads for an excellent broth in which to cook fillets of fish or prawns.

QUICK BOLOGNAISE SAUCE

SERVES 4 • PREPARATION: 5 MINUTES • COOKING: 30 MINUTES

1 tablespoon olive oil
2 onions
1 garlic clove
100 g (3½ oz) pancetta, cut into small pieces, or bacon lardons
250 g (8 oz) minced beef
400 g (14 oz) tinned tomatoes
1 teaspoon tomato paste
4 basil stalks
salt and freshly ground pepper

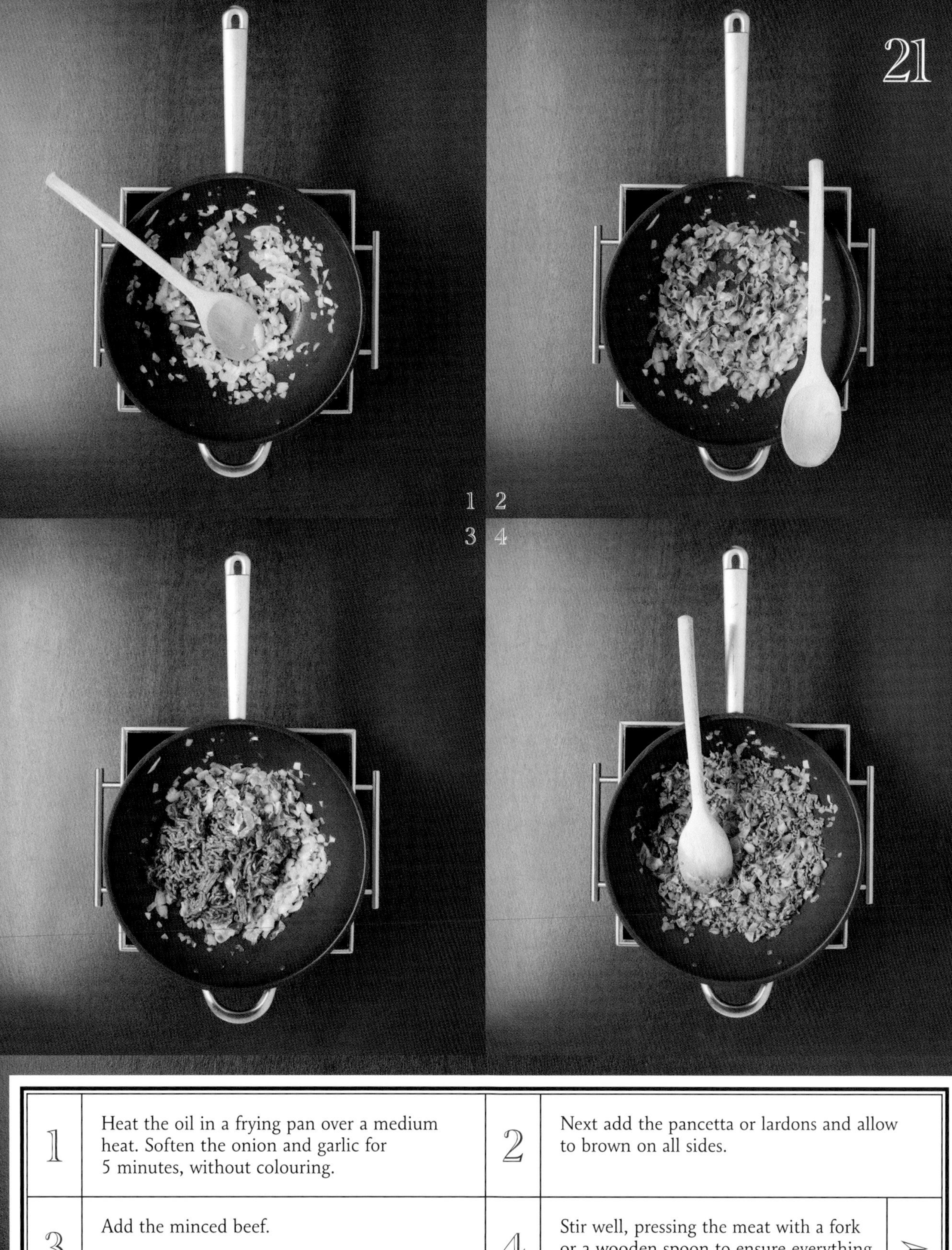

1	Heat the oil in a frying pan over a medium heat. Soften the onion and garlic for 5 minutes, without colouring.	2	Next add the pancetta or lardons and allow to brown on all sides.	
3	Add the minced beef.	4	Stir well, pressing the meat with a fork or a wooden spoon to ensure everything is broken up and evenly cooked.	➢

5	Add the tinned tomatoes, the tomato paste and the basil leaves. Season with salt and pepper and mix well.

NOTE

Tomato paste is not essential but it does add to the depth of flavour.

IN SUMMER

Use fresh tomatoes instead, skinned (first plunge them into boiling water for 1–2 minutes, then slip off the skins) and quartered.

IN WINTER

Select good-quality tinned tomatoes; usually the Italian ones. Check the ingredients to see if they include acidifiers; those in rich juice only are best.

6 Cover the pan and allow to bubble gently for 20 minutes over a low heat.

VARIATIONS

Instead of beef you can use sausagemeat, which children love. Or you can add a glass of hearty red wine at the same time as the tomatoes.

SERVING IDEAS

Serve this sauce over tagliatelle, spaghetti or layered in a lasagne and topped with béchamel sauce. Use it to stuff marrow or large courgettes and roast in the oven for 25 minutes at 200°C (400°F), Gas Mark 6. Sprinkle with Parmesan and put in the oven for a further 10 minutes.

ROCKET PESTO

SERVES 4–6 • PREPARATION: 10 MINUTES

100 g (3½ oz) rocket leaves
1 or 2 garlic cloves
2 tablespoons pine nuts
salt

25 g (1 oz) grated Parmesan or very dry Pecorino cheese
75 ml (3 fl oz) olive oil

CLASSIC PESTO:
Instead of rocket use basil, of course!

FOR A MORE UNUSUAL PESTO:
Use small tender dandelion leaves.

1	Use a pestle and mortar to crush the rocket leaves with the garlic, the pine nuts and a little salt.	**TIPS** Toast the pine nuts for 4–5 minutes in the top of a very hot oven. For preference use green (fresh) garlic which has a more subtle flavour. Use large grain salt or salt flakes if you can. The coarseness makes it easier to grind all the ingredients in the mortar.	➢

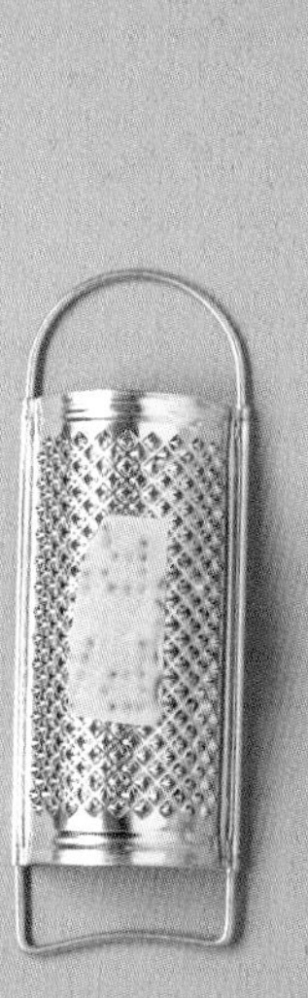

		TOOLS & EQUIPMENT
2	Add the grated cheese.	Using a pestle and mortar requires more effort but gives a better texture than using a blender. Work in batches if your pestle and mortar is a small one. The best pestles and mortars are the heaviest: in stone (try Indian stores), in marble and sometimes in metal. Wooden ones are less effective.
3	Add the oil, first drop by drop, then in a thin stream, as if making mayonnaise.	

4	The pesto is ready to serve.

STORING

The pesto will keep for a few days in the fridge stored in a well-sealed jar.

NOTE

For a lighter version you can reduce the amount of olive oil. However, if you want to keep the pesto in the fridge for a few days, you will need to cover it with a layer of oil to protect it from oxidation.

GOATS' CHEESE & PESTO TOASTS

VARIATION ON ROCKET PESTO

Spread the pesto on a toasted slice of country-style bread and top with fresh goats' cheese.

OTHER IDEAS:
This is also very good with fresh or sun-dried tomatoes.

You can use whole slices of bread or make mini toasts (sliced baguette) to go with an aperitif.

PISTACHIO PESTO

VARIATION ON ROCKET PESTO

Put 100 g (3½ oz) rocket leaves, 1 or 2 garlic cloves, a pinch of salt, 2 tablespoons pistachios and 75 ml (3 fl oz) oil in a food-processor.

Pulse until all the ingredients are fully blended. Transfer the pesto to a small bowl and add 25 g (1 oz) grated Parmesan.

NOTE:
The pistachios give a lovely green colour, but you can equally use walnuts, hazelnuts, almonds…

25

SPAGHETTI WITH TOMATO SAUCE

SERVES 2 • PREPARATION: 5 MINUTES • COOKING: 10 MINUTES

about 200 g (7 oz) dry spaghetti (according to appetite)
salt

200–300 g (7–10 fl oz) Tomato Sauce (see recipe 20) or Bolognaise Sauce (see recipe 21)
grated Parmesan to serve

1

2

3

4

5

6

1	Bring a large pan of salted water to the boil – allow 1 litre (1¾ pints) water to each 100 g (3½ oz) pasta.	2	When the water reaches a rolling boil, add the spaghetti and bring back to a full boil.	3	One or 2 minutes before the end of the cooking time indicated on the packet, test a strand to see if it is cooked.
4	Drain the spaghetti when it is al dente.	5	Stir the sauce into the spaghetti and mix well.	6	Serve the spaghetti sprinkled with Parmesan.

SPINACH & SQUASH LASAGNE

SERVES 4 • PREPARATION: 30 MINUTES • COOKING: 1 HOUR 30 MINUTES

2 small squash (butternut, buttercup or acorn are good choices)
500 g (1 lb) baby spinach
20 g (¾ oz) butter + extra for greasing
salt and freshly ground pepper
pinch of cayenne pepper
250 g (8 oz) precooked dried lasagne
500 ml (17 fl oz) Tomato Sauce (see recipe 20) or ready-made tomato coulis
200 g (7 oz) ricotta
300 ml (½ pint) Béchamel Sauce (see recipe 06)
40 g (1½ oz) Parmesan

IN ADVANCE:
Preheat the oven to 200°C (400°F), Gas Mark 6.

1	Put the squash in a roasting tin and bake in the oven for 40–50 minutes.	2	Meanwhile, wash the spinach leaves, destalk and pick them over.	3	Put the spinach in a pan over a medium heat. Add half the butter, salt and the cayenne.	
4	Cover the pan and leave the spinach to wilt for 5 minutes.	5	Remove the squash from the oven and cut in half. Scrape out the seeds and fibre.	6	Tip the flesh into a bowl and mash in some seasoning.	➢

7 8
9 10

7	Reduce the oven temperature to 180°C (350°F), Gas Mark 6. Butter a rectangular ovenproof dish. Line the base with a layer of lasagne.	8	Cover the lasagne with half the puréed squash then half the spinach.
9	Follow this with a layer of tomato sauce then crumble over half the ricotta.	10	Repeat the layers, first lasagne, then vegetables, tomato sauce and the ricotta. Finish with a third layer of lasagne then pour over the béchamel and sprinkle with Parmesan shavings.

11 Bake in the oven for 30 minutes.

STORING

The lasagne freezes very well.

ABOUT BUTTERNUT SQUASH

Butternut is an elongated squash with a bulbous end, skin the colour of egg yolk and orange flesh. It has become very popular, but try other squash, too.

27

PASTA WITH LEMON & CREAM

SERVES 4 • PREPARATION: 5 MINUTES • COOKING: 15 MINUTES

1 lemon
400 g (13 oz) short pasta

50 g (2 oz) salted butter
200 ml (7 fl oz) whipping cream, full- or reduced-fat

salt and freshly ground pepper
65 g (2½ oz) Parmesan

1 2
3 4

1	Rind the lemon and squeeze the juice. Measure off 2 tablespoons of juice.	2	Cook the pasta according to the instructions on the packet.
3	Melt the butter in a small saucepan over a low heat. Add the cream, season, then add the lemon rind and juice. Bring gently to the boil and allow to cook for 2 minutes.	4	Drain and mix the pasta with the sauce and serve sprinkled with grated or shaved Parmesan.

STIR-FRIED 'PAD THAI' NOODLES

SERVES 2 • PREPARATION: 20 MINUTES • COOKING: 5 MINUTES

150 g (5 oz) tofu
1 garlic clove and 2 spring onions
1 small carrot
125 g (4 oz) flat soya bean or rice noodles
2 tablespoons peanuts
4 tablespoons vegetable oil
2 tablespoons rice or white wine vinegar
2 tablespoons soy sauce
1½ teaspoons sugar
2 eggs
handful of beansprouts
2 large mint sprigs

1 2

3 4

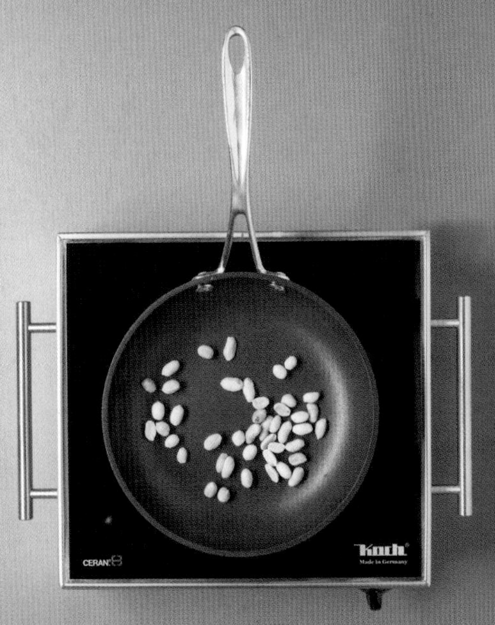

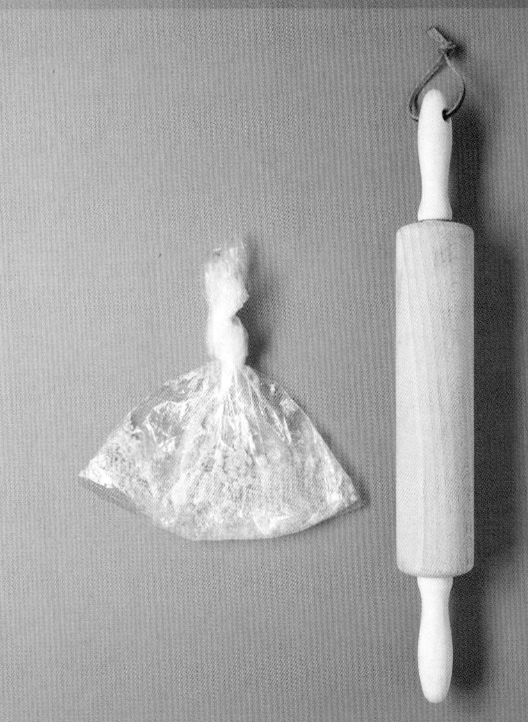

1	Cut the tofu into dice. Peel and finely chop the garlic. Trim and finely chop the spring onions. Peel and grate the carrot.	2	Cover the noodles with cold water, leave them to soak for 10 minutes then drain.	
3	Dry-roast the peanuts in a hot frying pan, shaking them constantly until they are golden.	4	Transfer the peanuts to a large plastic bag and crush them with a rolling pin or a glass bottle.	➢

5 6
7 8

5	Heat a wok over a very high heat. Add the oil and fry the tofu, stirring constantly until the cubes are browned on all sides.	6	Add the garlic, noodles, carrot, vinegar, soy sauce and sugar and 100 ml (3½ fl oz) water, stirring all the time.
7	Push these ingredients to the sides of the wok. Crack the eggs into the wok. Stir them to break the yolks then gradually incorporate them into the noodle mixture.	8	Allow to cook for 2–3 minutes, stirring and shaking the wok.

9	Share out between 2 plates. Sprinkle with the crushed peanuts and arrange the beansprouts and mint sprigs on the side.	**SERVING SUGGESTION** Serve with sweet chilli sauce if you like it. **VARIATIONS** In place of tofu you can use strips of chicken breast or peeled prawns.

SPICED PILAF RICE

SERVES 2 • PREPARATION: 15 MINUTES • COOKING: 20 MINUTES • RESTING: 5 MINUTES

seeds from 3 cardamom pods
pinch of cumin seeds
pinch of coriander seeds

1 tablespoon oil
1 onion, chopped
200 g (7 oz) basmati rice

1 cinnamon stick
6–7 dried apricots, chopped
salt

1 2
3 4

1	Crush the cardamom, cumin and coriander seeds using a pestle and mortar (or put them on a chopping board and crush them with the base of a heavy jar).	2	Heat a small saucepan or frying pan over a fairly high heat and dry-roast the crushed seeds for about 1 minute, or until the spices release their aroma.	
3	Heat the oil in another pan, add the chopped onion and cook over a medium heat for 5 minutes.	4	Add the roast spices and stir.	➢

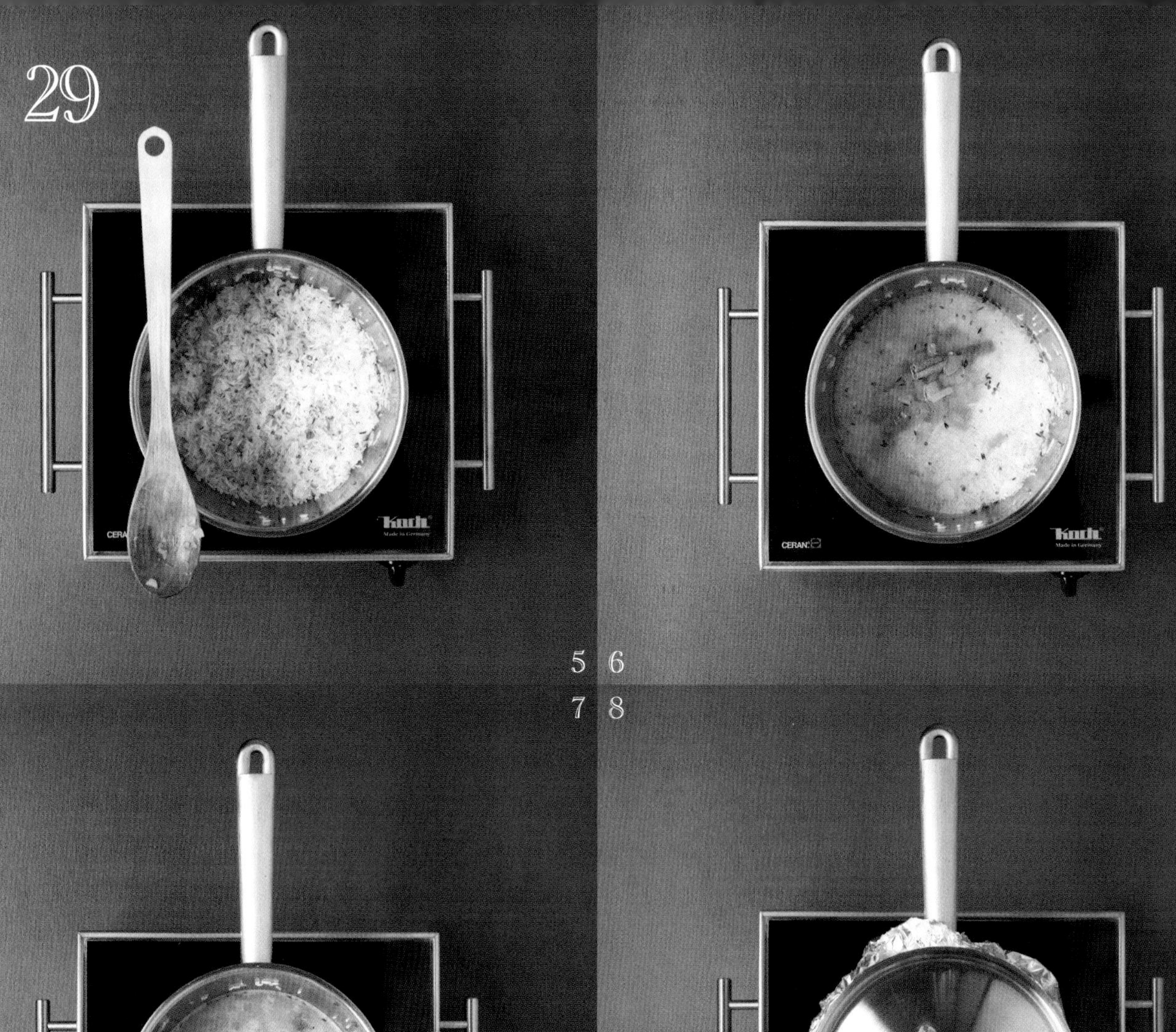

5 6
7 8

5	Add the rice and stir thoroughly with a wooden spoon until all the grains are coated and glistening with oil.	6	Pour in 375 ml (13 fl oz) water. Add the cinnamon stick and the chopped apricots.
7	Bring to the boil, add a pinch of salt and stir once.	8	Cover the pan with a lid. If it is not tight-fitting, put a sheet of aluminium foil between the pan and the lid.

9	Reduce the heat to a minimum and leave the pilaf to cook for 11 minutes without once lifting the lid. At the end of cooking, remove the pan from the heat, take off the lid and place a clean tea towel over the rice. Allow to rest for 5 minutes then remove the cinnamon stick. Fork through the rice to fluff it up and serve immediately.	**VARIATIONS** For golden rice, add a pinch of saffron threads to the hot water before covering the pan with the lid. For a non-spicy pilaf, simple follow the method omitting the spices and apricots. You can, of course, also leave out the onion.

RISOTTO PRIMAVERA

SERVES 2 • PREPARATION: 5 MINUTES • COOKING: 30 MINUTES

50 g (2 oz) butter
150 g (5 oz) spring vegetables (such as broad beans, peas, asparagus tips)
1 onion or 2 shallots, chopped

1 litre (1¾ pints) vegetable or chicken stock
200 g (7 oz) risotto rice (arborio, carnaroli)
½ glass white wine
40 g (1½ oz) freshly grated Parmesan

1 tablespoon crème fraîche or mascarpone, or use an extra 15 g (½ oz) butter
salt and freshly ground pepper

1	Melt half the butter in a heavy-based saucepan or casserole. Add the vegetables and cook them, stirring, over a medium heat for 2 minutes. Remove and set aside.	2	Melt the remaining butter in the pan. Add the onion and cook for 5 minutes over a medium heat. Separately, reheat the stock.	
3	Add the rice and stir thoroughly with a wooden spoon until all the grains are coated and glistening with oil.	4	Add the wine and allow to boil until all the liquid is absorbed by the rice.	➢

5	Add a ladleful of hot stock and stir until this too has been absorbed.	6	Return the vegetables to the pan.
7	Add the remaining stock, ladle by ladle, stirring until it is absorbed before adding the next ladleful. This will take 15–20 minutes.	8	Once the rice is cooked to a creamy perfection, add the Parmesan and mascarpone (or crème fraîche or butter) and beat with the spoon.

9	Check the seasoning and adjust if necessary (the stock will already be salted). Serve at once.

THE RIGHT RICE

Make sure you choose an Italian-style rice, that is, round grain.

THE RIGHT TOOL

A wooden spoon with a hole in it is ideal for preparing risotto, allowing you to stir without the rice sticking to the spoon. But you can succeed without it!

NOTE

☛ The amount of stock needed will depend on how quickly the rice absorbs it. Taste as you go and stop when the mixture is creamy but the rice still al dente.

MEAT

3

ROASTS

STEWS

WORLD

31

ROAST BEEF

✣ **SERVES 6** • PREPARATION: 5 MINUTES • COOKING: 1 HOUR ✣

1 kg (2 lb) sirloin or rib of beef, rolled and tied
1 small onion, peeled and quartered
2 tablespoons flour
salt and freshly ground pepper
1 litre (1¾ pints) vegetable stock made with 2 stock cubes

IN ADVANCE:
Preheat the oven to 220°C (425°F), Gas Mark 7. Select a deep roasting tin that will comfortably accommodate the beef.

1 2

3 4

1	Put the beef in the roasting tin. Arrange the onion quarters against the sides of the meat. Sprinkle the strip of fat on the beef with a little of the flour, and with salt and pepper.	2	Transfer the tin to the oven. Baste the beef several times with the juices as it cooks.
3	Roast for 30 minutes for rare meat, 45 minutes for medium.	4	Remove the beef from the oven, place on a board and cover loosely with aluminium foil to keep hot. ➢

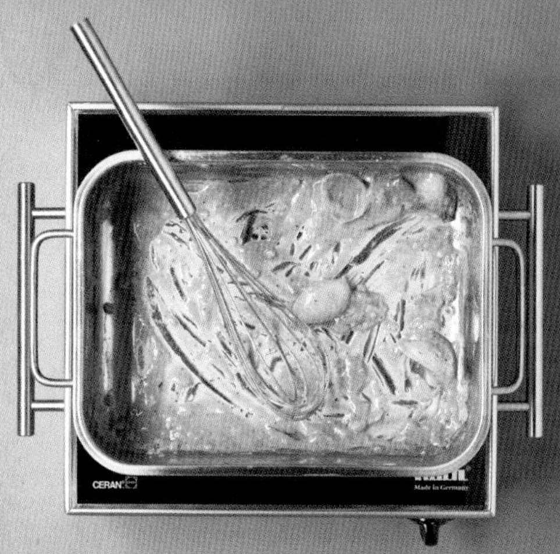

5 6

7 8

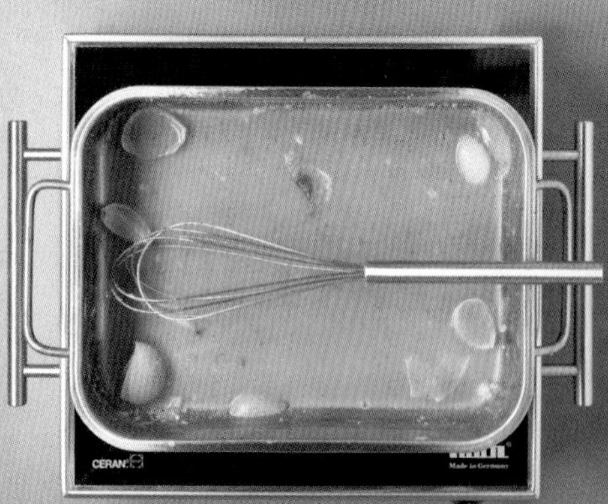

5	To make a gravy, place the roasting tin on the hob over a medium heat.	6	Sprinkle the remaining flour into the tin and use a whisk to incorporate the flour.
7	Heat the stock and add a little at a time to the pan, whisking constantly. Bring to the boil then allow to reduce over a gentle heat for about 5 minutes.	8	Taste and season as necessary.

9 Serve the beef with the gravy.

HORSERADISH CREAM

Mix together 2 tablespoons grated horseradish (sold in jars), 1 tablespoon crème fraîche, ½ teaspoon mustard, salt and freshly ground pepper.

SERVING SUGGESTIONS

Accompany the roast beef with mashed potato or a creamy potato gratin and, in spring, some asparagus stalks drizzled with a little olive oil and roasted in the oven for 20 minutes.

ROAST LAMB

SERVES 6 • PREPARATION: 10 MINUTES • COOKING: 1 HOUR 20 MINUTES

2 kg (4 lb) shoulder or leg of lamb
1 head of garlic
6 thyme stalks + 3 rosemary stalks
2 tablespoons olive oil
salt and pepper

IN ADVANCE:
Preheat the oven to 230°C (450°F), Gas Mark 8. Rinse the herbs and remove the leaves from 3 of the thyme stalks and 1 rosemary stalk. Chop the leaves finely.

COOKING TIME:
Depending on the weight of the joint, allow 20 minutes plus 15 minutes for every 500 g (1 lb).

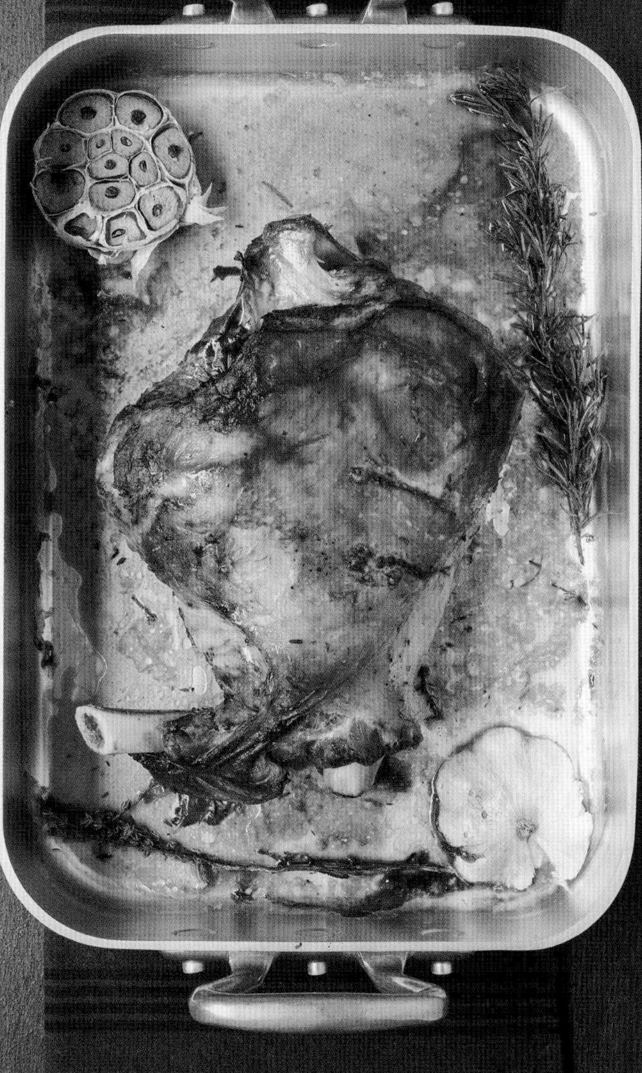

PREPARATION	COOKING
Put the lamb joint in a large roasting tin. Cut the garlic head in half and add to the pan. Arrange the whole stalks of thyme and rosemary around the meat. Mix the chopped herb leaves with the oil and a little salt and pepper and spread this mixture over the lamb.	Transfer the tin to the oven for 20 minutes, then lower the temperature to 200°C (400°F), Gas Mark 6. Cook for 1 hour for slighly pink meat. Remove the lamb from the oven, cover with aluminium foil and allow to rest for 10 minutes before serving.

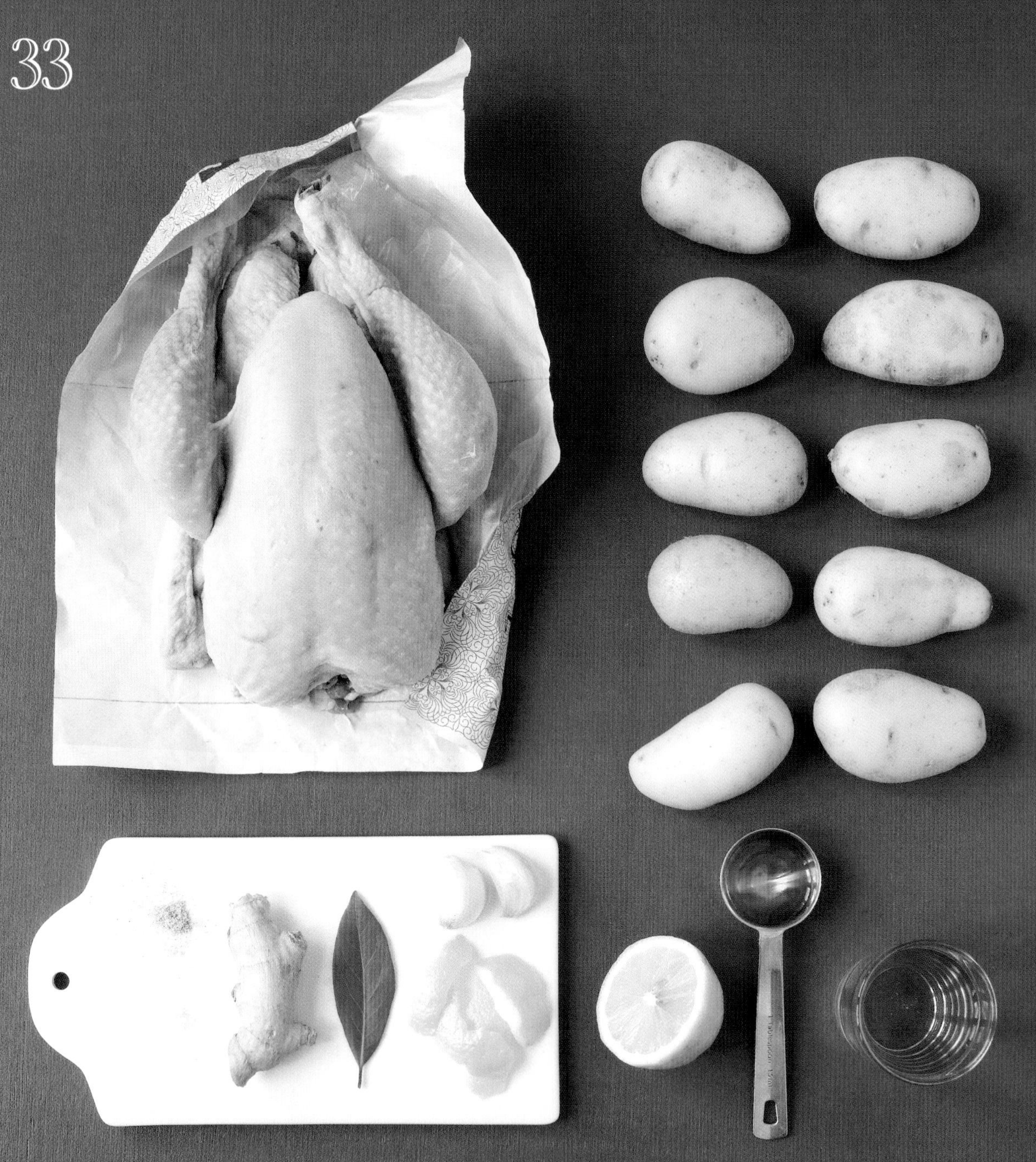

ROAST CHICKEN

SERVES 4 • PREPARATION: 15 MINUTES • COOKING: 1 HOUR 30 MINUTES

1 good-size roasting chicken (about 1.5 kg/3 lb)
1 lemon
1 knob of root ginger (about 5 cm/2 in)
1 tablespoon olive oil
1–2 garlic cloves
10 medium potatoes
1 glass of white wine

IN ADVANCE:
Preheat the oven to 200°C (400°F), Gas Mark 6.

1

Put the chicken in a large, deep-sided roasting tin. Use a paring knife to remove 4–5 wide strips of rind from the lemon. Peel the ginger and cut into thin slices. Slip the pared lemon rind and the ginger slices under the skin of the breast of the chicken.

Rub the olive oil over the chicken using your hands. Cut the lemon in two, crush the garlic cloves and place everything in the cavity of the chicken. Transfer the roasting tin to the oven.

➢

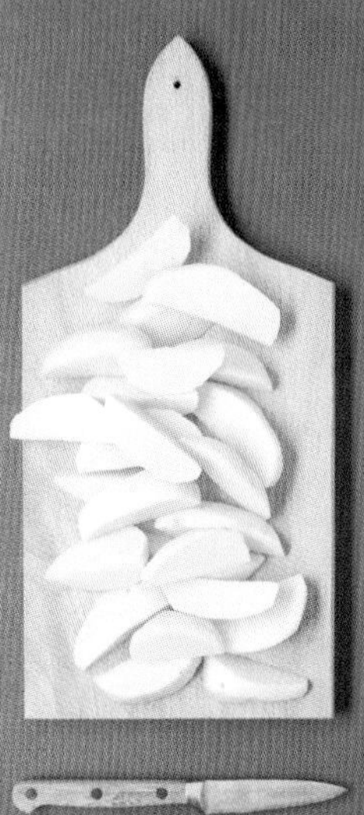

2 3

4 5

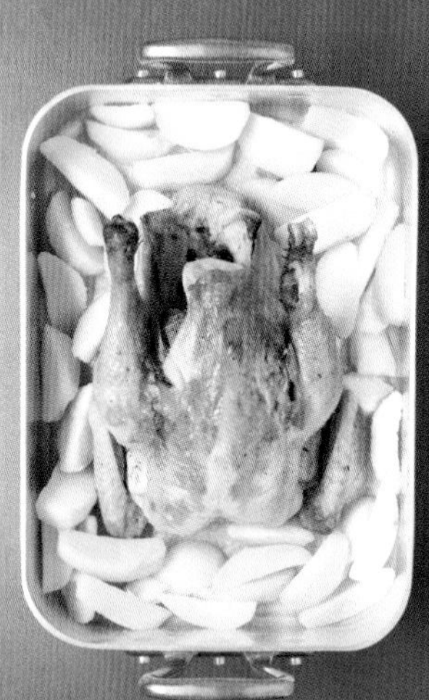

2	Meanwhile peel the potatoes and cut them into large chips.	3	Cook them for 10 minutes in a large saucepan of boiling water. Drain, then shake them a little in the pan.
4	After 45 minutes, turn over the chicken and baste with the juices.	5	Arrange the potatoes around the sides of the roasting tin. They will be crisp and golden at the same time as the chicken.

6	The chicken is cooked when it is golden all over and the thighs come away from the body almost of their own accord.	**TIP** ✲ If you like your breast meat moist, you can begin cooking the chicken upside down: simply place it breast-side down. This way, the fat will run into the breast and make it less dry.	➢

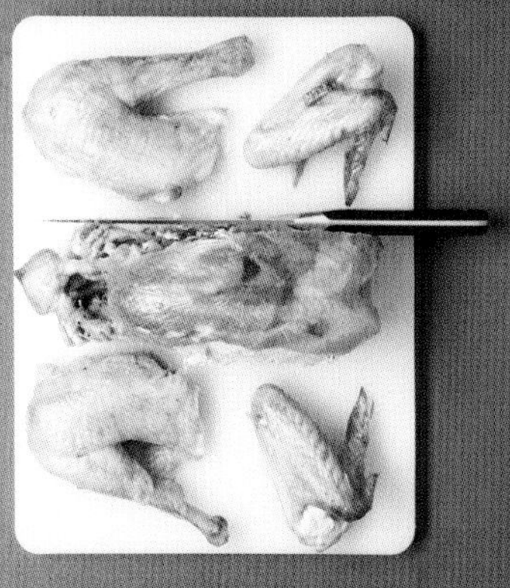

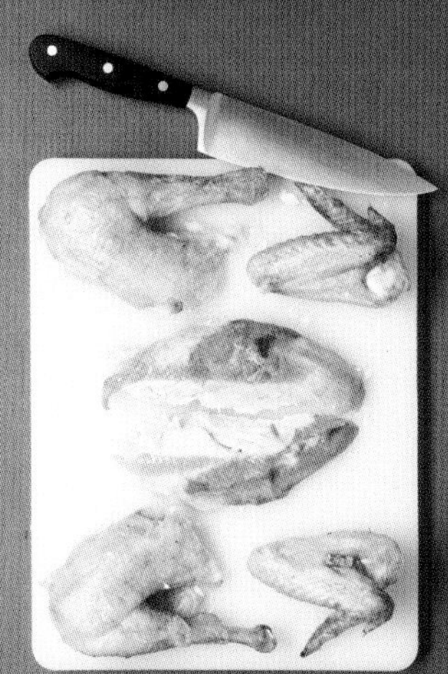

7 8

9 10

7	To carve the bird, transfer to a board and start by removing the thighs with a sharp knife.	8	Next remove the two breasts, then the wings.
9	To make the gravy, remove the potatoes and keep warm. Put the tin on the hob. Spoon off the excess fat then add the white wine along with the lemon halves and garlic from the bird.	10	Bring to the boil, scraping all the bits from the base of the tin and pressing the garlic and lemon with the back of a wooden spoon. Allow to reduce, then discard the garlic and lemon.

11 Serve the chicken with the potatoes and the gravy.

SERVING SUGGESTION

Serve with sliced courgettes, drizzled with olive oil and a little salt then roasted for 20 minutes in a hot oven, 200°C (400°F), Gas Mark 6.

FURTHER IDEAS

The following day, you can make a salad with raw grated vegetables, chopped apple, raisins and a vinaigrette enlivened with a pinch of curry powder and some thick yogurt stirred into it. Serve with the leftover chicken.

GUINEAFOWL & STUFFING

SERVES 6 • PREPARATION: 20 MINUTES • COOKING: 2 HOURS

625 g (1¼ lb) wild mushrooms (such as ceps, girolles), fresh or frozen
100 g (3½ oz) foie gras
1 chicken breast
6 flat leaf parsley stalks, 1 rosemary stalk
2 slices of white bread
100 ml (3½ fl oz) whipping cream
1 egg
salt and pepper
2 guineafowl
6 thin smoked bacon rashers
25 g (1 oz) butter

IN ADVANCE:
Preheat the oven to 200°C (400°F), Gas Mark 6.

1	Begin by making the stuffing. Chop 100 g (3½ oz) of the mushrooms, the foie gras, chicken breast and the herbs.	2	Soak the bread in the cream. Mix the chopped ingredients with the soaked bread and cream and the egg. Season with salt and pepper.	
3	Place the birds in a large roasting tin and fill the cavities with stuffing. Put the remaining stuffing in the tin alongside the birds.	4	Lay 3 rashers of bacon over the breast of each guineafowl.	➢

5	Slice the remaining mushrooms.	6	Heat the butter in a frying pan over a medium-high heat. Add the mushrooms and brown for 6–7 minutes.
7	Transfer the roasting tin to the oven. Baste the guineafowl halfway through cooking.	8	Cook for 1 hour 30 minutes to 2 hours, depending on the weight of your birds: check the label or ask your butcher.

9 Serve the guineafowl with the extra stuffing and mushrooms.

FOR GRAVY

Put the roasting tin on the hob over a medium heat, add a glass of white wine (dry or sweet), scrape off the bits from the base, bring to the boil, then reduce.

FOR CHRISTMAS

For a stuffing that is 100 per cent Christmas, add 100 g (3½ oz) chopped chestnuts (sold vacuum sealed). Or, for a traditional Christmas dinner, serve with Brussels sprouts steamed then turned in hot butter and mixed with the whole chestnuts.

35

BEEF BRAISED IN BEER

SERVES 4–6 • PREPARATION: 15 MINUTES • COOKING: 3 HOURS

2 onions cut into rings
2 garlic cloves, finely chopped
6 carrots, peeled and sliced
2 tablespoons olive oil
1 kg (2 lb) braising steak, cut into large cubes

1 tablespoon flour
450 ml (¾ pint) beer
2 thyme stalks
1 bay leaf
salt and freshly ground pepper

IN ADVANCE:
Preheat the oven to 140°C (275°F), Gas Mark 1. Prepare all the vegetables.

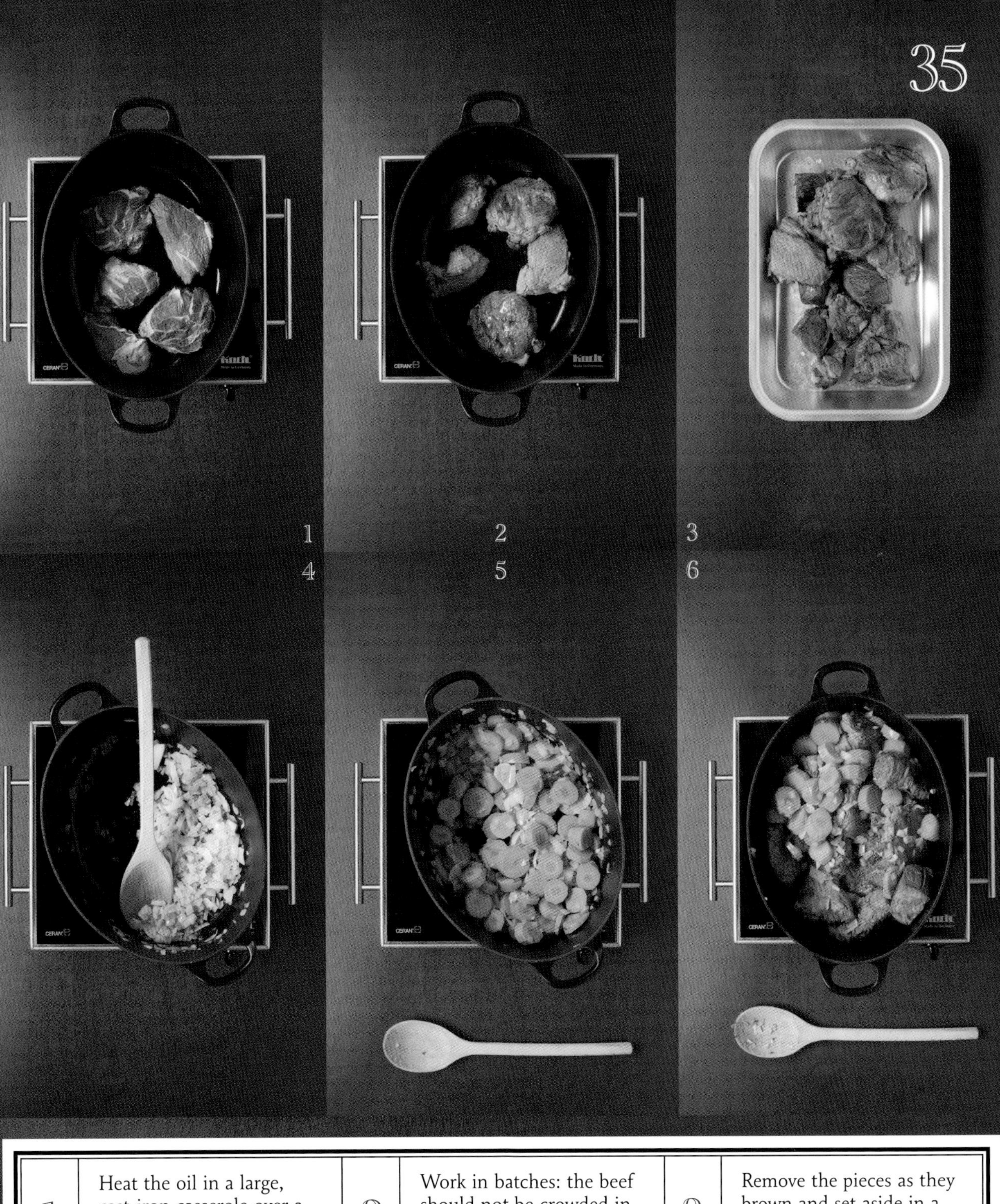

1	Heat the oil in a large, cast-iron casserole over a high heat. Add the beef and brown on both sides.	2	Work in batches: the beef should not be crowded in the casserole if it is to brown evenly.	3	Remove the pieces as they brown and set aside in a roasting tin.
4	Brown the onions in the casserole for 4–5 minutes over a medium-high heat.	5	Add the garlic and the carrots and stir everything for 1 minute.	6	Return the meat to the casserole. ➢

7	Stir in the flour. Reduce the heat.

NOTE

The flour will thicken the gravy.

VARIATION 1

To make a goulash, add 1 tablespoon of paprika with the flour. Omit the beer and add a large tin of chopped tomatoes then, 30 minutes before the cooking time is up, add 1 chopped red pepper.

8

Add the beer, the thyme and the bay leaf and bring gently to a simmer.

VARIATION 2

For beef bourguignon, simply use red wine instead of the beer.

35

9 Cover the pan tightly and transfer to the oven for 2–3 hours.

LONG AND SLOW

You could also leave the casserole in the oven for longer at a lower temperature. In this instance, the temperature does not have to be precise.

ON THE HOB

You can also cook the casserole on the hob but make sure the heat is turned down to a minimum.

10 The meat is cooked when it starts to fall apart. Serve with boiled potatoes and a green salad.

OPTION

Add some mushrooms 30 minutes before the end of the cooking time.

TIP

This stew is actually better served the following day or the day after. To reheat: put the casserole back in a preheated oven at 160°C (325°F), Gas Mark 3 for 40 minutes or place over a medium heat, bring to a gentle simmer and heat for 30 minutes.

POT-AU-FEU

✧ SERVES 4 • PREPARATION: 15 MINUTES • COOKING: 4 HOURS ✧

1 kg (2 lb) stewing steak
3 large or 6 small carrots
4 large leeks, washed and trimmed
1 celery stick, washed
1 onion, peeled

2 garlic cloves, peeled
3 turnips
1 bouquet garni
peppercorns + coarsegrain salt
6–10 potatoes, peeled

SUGGESTED CONDIMENTS:
mustard
small gherkins
tomato sauce

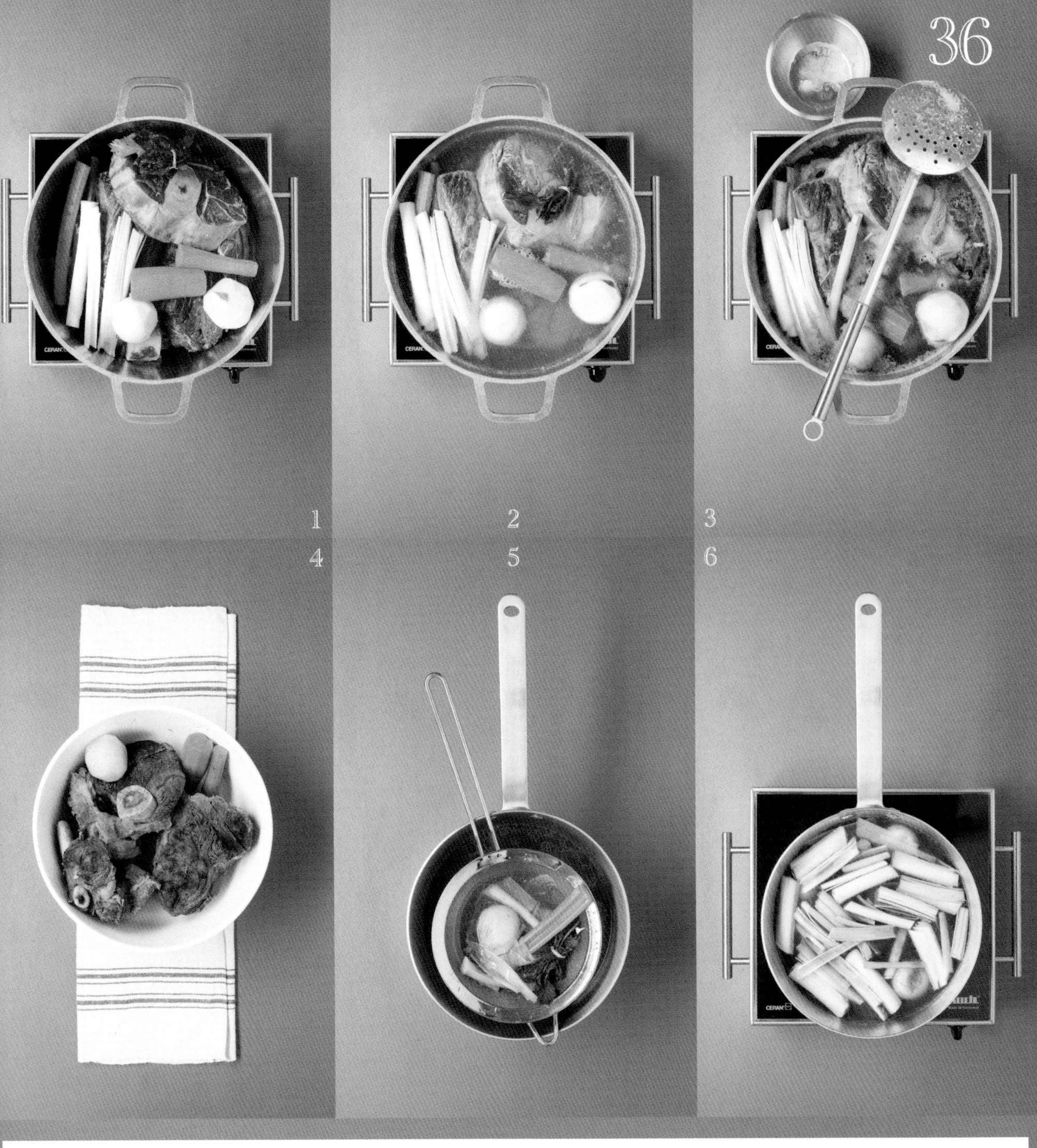

1	Put the meat, 1 carrot, 2 leeks, celery, onion, garlic, 2 turnips, bouquet garni and peppercorns in a stockpot.	2	Cover with water and bring gently to simmering point.	3	Leave to cook gently bubbling for 3–4 hours, occasionally skimming the foam from the surface.	
4	At the end of cooking, lift out the meat and the vegetables.	5	Pour the stock through a strainer into a saucepan and discard the flavourings.	6	Bring it to the boil, then add salt and the remaining vegetables.	➤

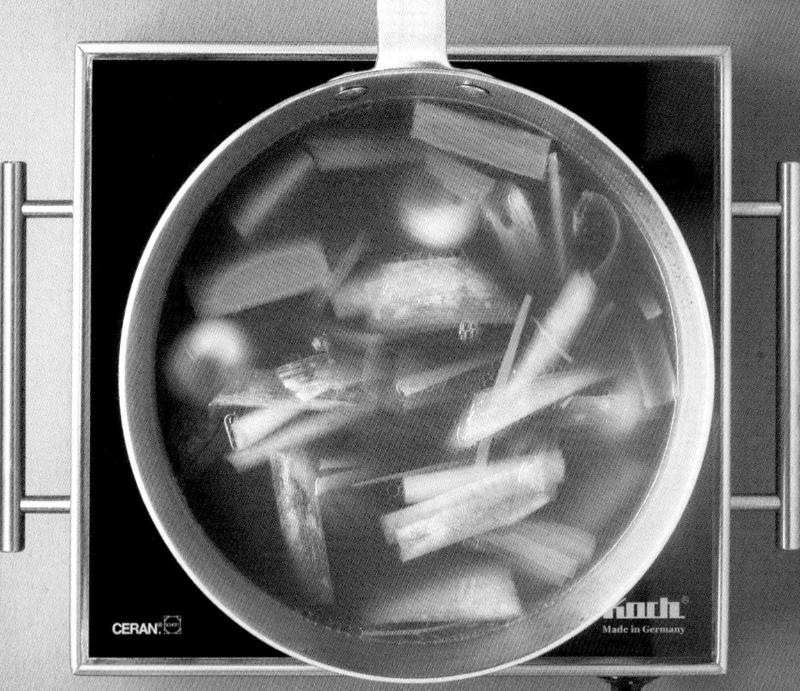

7	Cook for 15–20 minutes.

VARIATION

In spring you can vary the vegetables to take advantage of new season peas, green beans…

OTHER IDEAS

Serve the stock just as it is with the vegetables or use as the base for a soup. You could also cook little alphabet pasta in it.

8 Serve the stock, the meat and the vegetables with the condiments.

SALAD FOR THE DAY AFTER

Cut the meat and vegetables into small pieces. Serve with crunchy green salad leaves and chopped gherkins or with caperberries and tomatoes. Dress with a classic vinaigrette or the blue cheese version.

COTTAGE PIE

Chop any leftover meat and vegetables as finely as possible and spread in a layer over the base of a gratin dish. Cover with mashed potato, sprinkle with breadcrumbs and put in a preheated oven at 190°C (375°F), Gas Mark 5 for 20 minutes to brown.

VEAL STEW WITH THAI RICE

SERVES 4 • PREPARATION: 15 MINUTES • COOKING: 1 HOUR 15 MINUTES

1–1.2 kg (2–2½ lb) stewing veal, chopped
1 veal bone if your butcher has one
3 large leeks, trimmed
4–6 carrots, trimmed

1 onion, peeled and quartered
1 garlic clove
25 g (1 oz) butter + 1 tablespoon flour
1 vanilla pod

75 ml (3 fl oz) crème fraîche
½ lemon
300 g (10 oz) Thai rice
salt and pepper

1 2

3 4

1	Put the meat and bone (if using) with 1 leek, 1 carrot, the onion and garlic in a large cast-iron casserole.	2	Cover with water and bring to the boil. Reduce the heat to a gentle boil and cook, uncovered.	
3	After 30 minutes add the remaining vegetables.	4	After 15 minutes, strain the stock into a saucepan. Set the meat and vegetables to one side.	➢

37

5	Melt the butter in the casserole. Tip in the flour all at once and mix with the butter. Add a ladleful of stock, bring to the boil, whisking, then add 3–4 more ladlefuls of the stock.	6	Add the vanilla seeds scraped from the pod and the crème fraîche. Cook for 5 minutes over a very low heat then add a squeeze of lemon juice. Taste and adjust the seasoning.
7	Measure the rice in a cup. Rinse and put in a saucepan. Pour in 1.5 times the volume of cold water to rice. Bring to the boil, salt, and stir.	8	Remove from the heat, cover with a tightly fitting lid and leave for 20 minutes. Remove the lid and fork through the rice to fluff it up.

9	Return the meat and vegetables to the casserole, reheat in the sauce if necessary then serve with the rice.	**TIP** You can also cook the rice in the traditional way, for 11 minutes in boiling water, then drain.

RABBIT TAGINE

SERVES 4 • PREPARATION: 10 MINUTES • COOKING: 1 HOUR 15 MINUTES

1 rabbit, jointed (ask your butcher to do this)
750 ml (1¼ pints) prune juice
4 onions, peeled and chopped
2–3 tablespoons olive oil
1 knob of ginger (about 5 cm/2 in)
½ teaspoon paprika
1 teaspoon ras-el-hanout
pinch of saffron threads
1 cinnamon stick
salt and freshly ground pepper
12 prunes
6 sun-dried tomatoes (optional)
2 tablespoons honey
6 coriander stalks
6 flat leaf parsley stalks

1	Arrange the rabbit pieces in the tagine. Pour over the prune juice.	2	Add the chopped onion and the olive oil.	3	Peel then finely grate the ginger and add to the tagine.	
4	Finally, sprinkle in the paprika, ras-el-hanout and saffron and tuck in the cinnamon stick.	5	Bring gently to a simmer then lower the heat and season to taste with salt and pepper.	6	Cover and cook on a gentle heat for between 40 minutes and 1 hour.	➢

7	Add the prunes and the tomatoes (if using) and continue to cook, covered, for 15 minutes. Lastly, add the honey and cook for a further 10 minutes, uncovered.	**OPTION** Stir in 1 teaspoonful of orange flower water at the same time as the honey for an even more delectable flavour.

8 Taste and adjust the seasoning if necessary. Serve sprinkled with the chopped herbs.

CARE FOR YOUR TAGINE

Oil the tagine cooking pot before using.

USING THE TAGINE

On a gas hob: use a heat-diffusing mat. On electric and ceramic hobs: keep the heat very low. On halogen hobs: inadvisable, unless you have a cast-iron tagine. In the oven: at a very low temperature, 140°C (275°F), Gas Mark 1.

CHICKEN, OLIVE & LEMON TAGINE

VARIATION ON RABBIT TAGINE

Follow the previous recipe for tagine, replacing the rabbit with chicken pieces, the prunes with chopped preserved lemons and 15 olives. Use water instead of prune juice and ground cumin instead of ras-el-hanout. When you add the preserved lemon, slice 4–5 courgettes and put them in the tagine to cook for the last 15 minutes.

LAMB & PRUNE TAGINE

VARIATION ON RABBIT TAGINE

Follow the rabbit tagine recipe, replacing the rabbit with 1.2 kg (2½ lb) lamb fillet, cubed (or slices of leg of lamb) and use water instead of prune juice. To serve, sprinkle with the chopped herbs and 2 tablespoons of sesame seeds.

41

PORK MEATBALLS

SERVES 4 • PREPARATION: 20 MINUTES • RESTING: 1 HOUR • COOKING: 10 MINUTES

1 large white onion, or 4 spring onions
1 garlic clove
6 coriander stalks

100 g (3½ oz) pancetta or smoked bacon
500 g (1 lb) minced pork or sausagemeat
¼ teaspoon chinese five-spice

salt and freshly ground pepper
2 tablespoons oil

1 2

3 4

1	Put the peeled onion and garlic in the bowl of a food-processor with the coriander.	2	Mix until roughly chopped. (You can, of course, also do this by hand using a knife on a wooden board.)	
3	Chop the pancetta or bacon with a sharp cook's knife.	4	Mix everything with the minced pork, add the spices and salt and pepper. Cover and put in the fridge for 1 hour.	➢

5	Form the mixture into balls no larger than golf balls then flatten them slightly.	**VARIATIONS** ☛ To make a Thai-flavoured version: omit the five-spice and mix in instead the tender hearts of 2 lemon grass stalks, chopped very finely, and 1 small chilli, also choppped finely. These meatballs could be served in a rich chicken broth flavoured with lemon grass, ginger and lime.

6

Heat the oil in a frying pan over a medium-high heat. Brown the meatballs on both sides, allowing about 2 minutes on each side. Reduce the heat and leave to cook for a further 5 minutes. Serve with a little chilli sauce, salad, rice or pitta bread.

OPTIONAL SAUCE

☛ When you have cooked the meatballs, wipe out the pan and return it to the heat. Pour in 1 tablespoon of muscat wine, 2 tablespoons of soy sauce and 2 tablespoons of dry white wine and stir. Allow to reduce briefly then pour over the meatballs.

CHICKEN TIKKA KEBABS

SERVES 4 • PREPARATION: 20 MINUTES • COOKING: 20 MINUTES • RESTING: MINIMUM 1 HOUR

1 knob of ginger
1 garlic clove
2 pots (125 g/4 fl oz size) plain yogurt
½ teaspoon paprika

½–1 teaspoon garam masala
1 tablespoon lemon juice
½ teaspoon olive oil
salt

500 g (1 lb) chicken, use a mixture of breast and deboned thigh meat, cut into pieces
6 coriander stalks + ½ lemon

1 Peel and grate the ginger. Peel and finely chop the garlic. Mix together the ingredients for the marinade: the yogurt, ginger, paprika, garam masala, lemon, oil and a little salt.

SOURCING SPICES

Garam masala can be bought in Indian stores as well as supermarkets. You could use curry powder.

HOMEMADE GARAM MASALA

Heat a frying pan until hot then dry-roast 3 tablespoons coriander seeds, 2 tablespoons cumin seeds, the seeds from 5 cardamom pods, 5 cloves, 1 cinnamon stick, ½ tablespoon black peppercorns, 1 bay leaf and ¼ teaspoon grated nutmeg. Once they give off their aroma, tip into a mortar and grind to a powder.

➢

2	Place the chicken pieces in the marinade, stir to coat and leave to marinate for 1 hour (and up to 1 day) in the fridge.	**MARINATING TIME** This dish is not quite as good if you do not have time to marinate the chicken. The yogurt tenderizes the meat and the spices flavour it.

3	Preheat the grill or prepare a barbecue. Thread the chicken pieces onto metal skewers. Grill them for about 10 minutes on each side until they are golden brown all over.

COOKING

The kebabs are delicious cooked on a barbecue but wait until the flames have died down, otherwise you risk burning the marinade covering the chicken.

SERVING SUGGESTION

Enjoy the kebabs sprinkled with chopped coriander and a squeeze of lemon served with naan or pitta bread.

ANOTHER IDEA

These kebabs are also good served cold, for a picnic, perhaps.

➢

43

LIGHT MOUSSAKA

SERVES 4 • PREPARATION: 25 MINUTES • COOKING: 1 HOUR 10 MINUTES

2 large or 3 small aubergines
100 ml (3½ fl oz) olive oil
2 large lamb leg steaks, cut into pieces
3–4 tomatoes

6 flat leaf parsley stalks, leaves washed and stripped
2–3 slices of day-old bread for breadcrumbs
salt and pepper
¼ teaspoon ground cinnamon

300 ml (½ pint) Béchamel Sauce (see recipe 06)

IN ADVANCE:
Preheat the oven to 220°C (425°F), Gas Mark 7.

1 2 3

4 5 6

1	Wash the aubergines and cut them into slices about ½-cm (¼-in) thick.	2	Spread them out in a single layer on a baking sheet and brush them with 3 tablespoons of olive oil.	3	Roast the slices for 20–30 minutes. You may need to cook them in two batches.
4	Heat 1 tablespoon oil in a heavy frying pan. Cook the lamb over a medium heat.	5	Chop the cooked lamb into small pieces. Slice the tomatoes.	6	Chop the parsley, mix with the breadcrumbs and season. ➢

7	Oil a large tin. Build up layers of aubergines, meat and tomatoes, seasoning each layer. Cover with béchamel, breadcrumbs and sprinkle with oil.	**OPTION 1** If liked, add a layer of soft sheep's cheese (or Greek yogurt). For a vegetarian option, it can replace the meat.

IMPORTANT

☛ Between each layer you need to season with salt, pepper and cinnamon, for that true Greek flavour.

OPTION 2

You can of course use ready-prepared minced lamb, or beef or veal, for a less pronounced flavour.

8	Transfer to the oven and cook for 30 minutes. Serve with a green salad.

NOTE

☛ This modern take on the classic recipe for moussaka is neither too light nor too heavy.

OPTION 3

For a more authentic version use ready-prepared minced lamb, a good layer of tomato sauce and even a layer of boiled potatoes, cut into slices.

FISH & SHELLFISH

CLASSICS

PAN-FRIED

MARINATED

FISH PARCELS WITH 3 SAUCES

SERVES 4 • PREPARATION: 5 MINUTES • COOKING: 15 MINUTES

4 salmon steaks, each about 150 g (5 oz)
1 tablespoon olive oil
1 lemon, salt and freshly ground pepper

IN ADVANCE:
Preheat the oven to 200°C (400°F), Gas Mark 6.

HOW TO COOK IN PARCELS:
Place the salmon steaks on a large sheet of aluminium foil brushed with olive oil. Season with salt, pepper and a squeeze of lemon juice.

Wrap the steaks to completely seal but do not enclose them tightly: the hot air needs to circulate inside the parcel as they cook. Fold over all edges to seal the foil. Cook for 10–15 minutes.

44

1 2

3 4

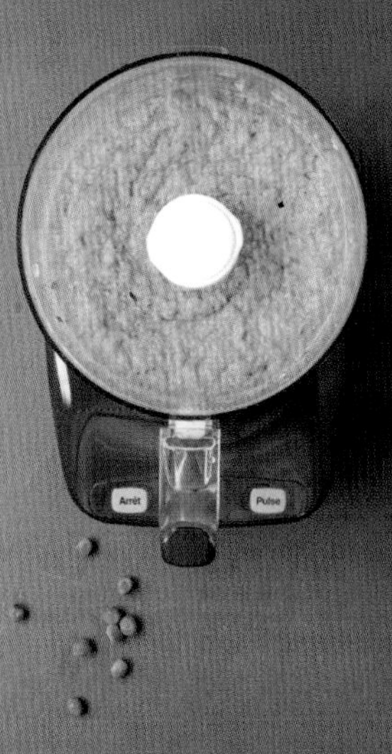

GREEN SAUCE

1 & 2 Roughly blend in a food processor: ½ bunch flat leaf parsley, 1 small red onion or 2 spring onions, 2 tarragon sprigs, 1 tablespoon capers, 2 tablespoons olive oil and 2 teaspoons wholegrain mustard.

YOGURT SAUCE

3 Mix together 6 finely chopped dill fronds with 2 individual pots Greek-style yogurt and 1 tablespoon lemon juice.

PEA & BASIL SAUCE

4 Blend together 450 g (14 oz) cooked peas with 6 basil stalks and 1 tablespoon olive oil.

45

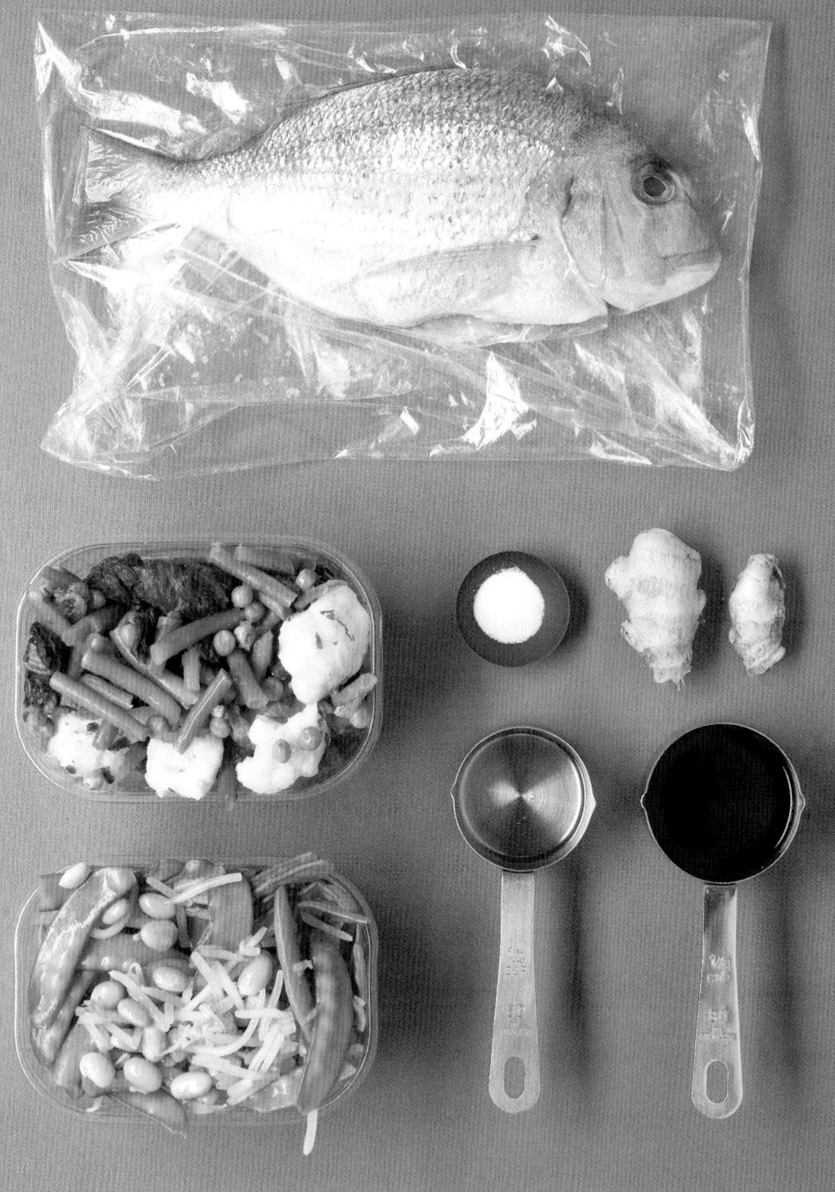

STEAMED VEGETABLES & FISH

SERVES 2 • PREPARATION: 10 MINUTES • COOKING: 20 MINUTES

2 small whole fish (sea bass or sea bream, for example)
1 knob of ginger, about 4–5 cm (1½–2 in) long
selection of spring vegetables
2 tablespoons oil
3 tablespoons soy sauce
pinch of sugar

IN ADVANCE:
Make diagonal cuts on both sides of the fish, through to the bone. Peel the ginger, cut half into fine slices and grate the remainder.

1 2

3 4

1	Place the fish in a steamer with the slices of ginger on top. Peel and cut the vegetables into short lengths and place them inside the steamer with the fish.	2	Steam for 12–15 minutes according to the thickness of the fish: once cooked, the flesh should flake easily.
3	Heat the oil in a small frying pan or saucepan. Add the grated ginger and stir around for 1 minute.	4	Remove the pan from the heat, add the soy sauce and the sugar. Pour over the fish and vegetables and serve.

BREADED FISH FILLETS

→ **SERVES 2** • PREPARATION: 20 MINUTES • COOKING: 10 MINUTES ←

2 slices dry bread
rind and juice of 1 lemon
1 bunch of herbs or a mixture, leaves stripped and washed
salt
25 g (1 oz) butter
2 fish fillets, not too thick (salmon, trout, sole…)

IN ADVANCE:
Preheat the oven to 200°C (400°F) Gas Mark 6.

1

2

3

4

5

6

1	Use a food-processor to reduce the bread to crumbs.	2	Add the lemon rind and the herbs and quickly reduce to a powder. Season with salt.	3	Melt the butter in a small saucepan and add the lemon juice.
4	Press the fish fillets in the breadcrumb mixture to coat both sides then transfer to a baking dish.	5	Sprinkle over the remaining breadcrumbs then pour the melted butter on top.	6	Cook for 6–10 minutes according to the thickness of the fillets. Serve with a little green salad.

MUSSELS WITH TARRAGON

SERVES 2 • PREPARATION: 10 MINUTES • COOKING: 10 MINUTES

2 litres (3½ pints) mussels, cleaned
25 g (1 oz) butter
2–3 shallots or 1 onion

1 glass of white wine
1 good long tarragon stalk with plenty of leaves

IN ADVANCE:
Clean the mussels in cold water with a small brush or knife. Discard any broken ones or those that remain open.

1	Melt the butter in a large lidded casserole. Finely chop the shallots. Cook gently in the butter for 5 minutes over a medium heat.	2	Increase the heat to high, then add the white wine and the tarragon.
3	Add the mussels, cover the pan tightly with the lid and allow to cook for 3–5 minutes, shaking the pan from time to time.	4	Serve immediately – with chips is traditional.

SCALLOPS WITH GARLIC & GINGER

SERVES 2 • PREPARATION: 10 MINUTES • COOKING: 10 MINUTES

8–10 prepared scallops off the shell
(or use frozen ones and defrost)
1 garlic clove and/or a small piece of ginger

6 fresh flat leaf parsley or coriander stalks
50 g (2 oz) butter

IN ADVANCE:
Defrost the scallops if using frozen. Spread them out on a dish and leave in the fridge for 4 hours.

1	Finely chop the garlic. Wash and dry the herbs, strip the leaves and chop finely.	2	Melt half the butter in a frying pan over a medium-high heat until it foams.	3	Add the scallops and cook for 2–3 minutes on one side.
4	Turn the scallops over and cook for 1–2 minutes on the second side. Remove to a plate. Discard the butter.	5	Melt the remaining butter until it foams. Add in the garlic, stir for 1 minute then add the herbs.	6	Pour the garlic and herb butter over the scallops and serve immediately.

TIGER PRAWNS & VANILLA SAUCE

SERVES 4 • PREPARATION: 10 MINUTES • COOKING: 10 MINUTES

VANILLA SAUCE:
250 ml (8 fl oz) vegetable or fish stock
5 tablespoons single or whipping cream
1 vanilla pod, split in two

2 tablespoons olive oil
16–20 whole tiger prawns, unshelled

1	First make the sauce. Pour the stock and cream into a small saucepan. Scrape the vanilla seeds into the pan and put in the pod too. Heat gently together.	2	Heat the olive oil in a large griddle pan or frying pan and fry the tiger prawns on one side for 2–3 minutes. Do not overcrowd the pan; work in batches if necessary.
3	Turn over the prawns and cook on the second side for 2 minutes.	4	Serve the prawns with the sauce.

JUST-COOKED TUNA STEAK

SERVES 2 • COOKING: 1 MINUTE

1 tablespoon olive oil
1 large (or 2 small) tuna steaks
either: soy sauce, wasabi, pickled ginger (sushi ginger)
or: 1 tablespoon wholegrain mustard
salt

1 2

3 4

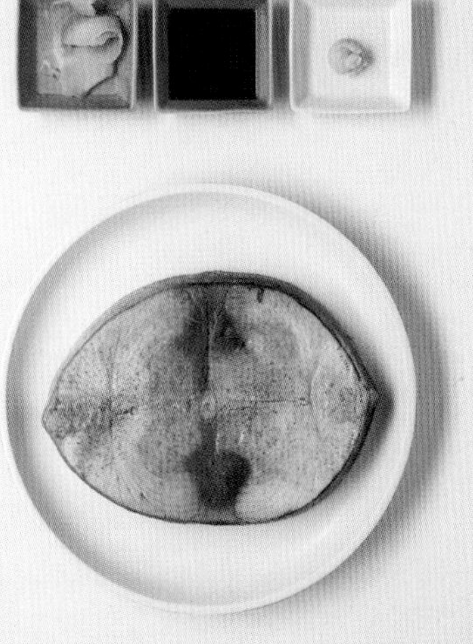

1	Heat the oil in a frying pan. Seal the tuna for just 30 seconds on one side.	2	Turn over the tuna and cook the second side for another 30 seconds.
3	Serve with Japanese condiments.	4	Alternatively, serve with whole-grain mustard and a little salt.

CEVICHE WITH LIME

SERVES 2 • PREPARATION: 15 MINUTES • CHILLING: 30 MINUTES

2 fillets of sea bass prepared by your fishmonger (the fish must be ultra-fresh)
4 tablespoons olive oil
1–2 limes
juice of 1 orange
1 fennel bulb
salt and pepper

1 2
3 4

1	Remove any bones from the fish fillets using your fingers or fish tweezers then cut the fillets into strips.	2	Put the fish into a non-metallic dish and pour over the oil.
3	Grate the rind of the limes and squeeze the juice. Mix with the orange juice. Wash and trim the fennel bulb then cut into fine slices.	4	Pour the juice and rind over the fish and add the fennel slices. Season with salt and pepper. Serve immediately or within a maximum of 30 minutes if you prefer the fish more 'cooked'.

TUNA TAHITIAN-STYLE

SERVES 4 • PREPARATION: 15 MINUTES • CHILLING: 30 MINUTES

4 small boneless tuna fillets (ask your fishmonger to debone them for you)
½ cucumber
2–3 limes
150–200 ml (5–7 fl oz) coconut milk
1 tablespoon olive oil
salt and freshly ground pepper
¼ bunch of fresh coriander

1 2
3 4

1	Cut the tuna into small cubes. Peel, deseed and grate the cucumber.	2	Grate the rind of 1 lime and squeeze the juice from 4 lime halves.
3	Mix together the ingredients for the marinade in a non-metallic dish: the cucumber, lime rind and juice, coconut milk and olive oil. Season with salt and pepper.	4	Put the tuna in the dish and sprinkle with chopped coriander. Serve immediately or within a maximum of 30 minutes if you prefer the tuna more 'cooked' in the lime juice.

VEGETABLES

SOUPS & CO.

BAKED VEGETABLES

ONE-POT VEGETABLES

RAW & SIMPLY COOKED

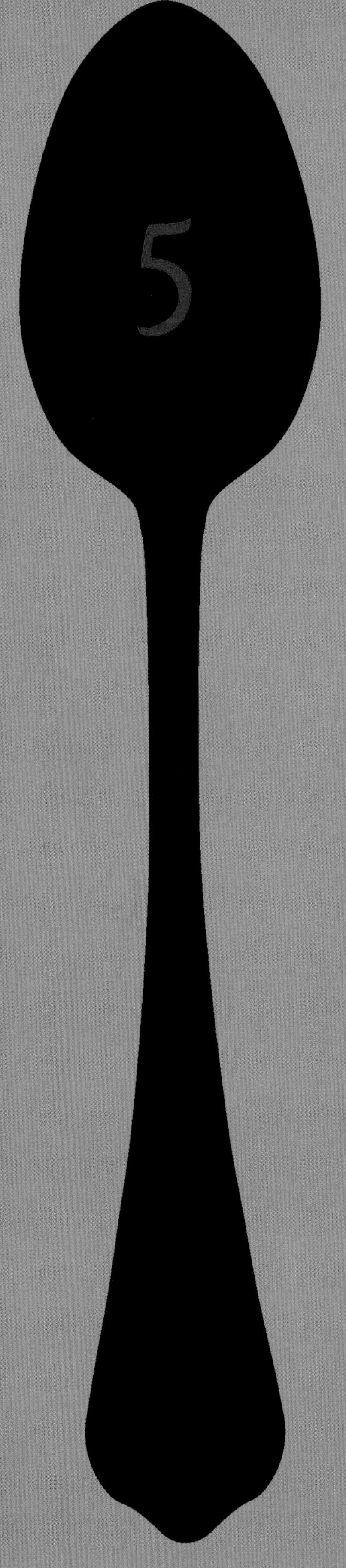

SQUASH SOUP

→ **SERVES 4** • PREPARATION: 25 MINUTES • COOKING: 1 HOUR ←

1 acorn squash or other variety
1 slice of pumpkin
3 potatoes
2 vegetable or chicken stock cubes

salt and freshly ground pepper
6 chervil stalks
4 tablespoons crème fraîche
or coconut milk

IN ADVANCE:
Preheat the oven to 200°C (400°F), Gas Mark 6.

1 2

3 4

1	Put the squash and the pumpkin, unpeeled, in an ovenproof dish. Roast for 30–40 minutes: the flesh should give when tested with a knife.	2	Remove the vegetables from the oven. Cut the squash in half, remove and discard the seeds and fibres. Scoop the flesh from the skins.	
3	While the squash and pumpkin are roasting, peel the potatoes, cut into pieces and place in a large saucepan. Cover them with water then add the stock cubes.	4	Bring to the boil and cook the potatoes for 20–25 minutes or until they are tender when tested with a knife.	➢

5	Put the squash and pumpkin flesh into the pan with the potatoes. Mix with a stick-blender (or transfer everything to a liquidizer, or pass through a mouli-légumes) until smooth and evenly blended. Check the seasoning and add salt and pepper if necessary. Chop the chervil.	**IF YOUR SOUP IS TOO THICK...** Stir in a little water, milk or extra stock. **OPTION** Squash and pumpkin go very well with ginger. If you wish, add a small piece of finely grated ginger before you blend the soup.

6	Serve the soup with a spoonful of cream or coconut milk in each bowl, and sprinkled with the chopped chervil.	**DE-LUXE VERSION** In place of the cream, top each bowl with shavings of foie gras before serving.

TIPS

You can use other varieties of squash, such as butternut, to make this soup. The potatoes help to thicken it, while offsetting the sweetness of the pumpkin.

FOR A MEAL IN ITSELF

Add some cubes of cheese, croûtons or cooked smoked lardons.

NEW STYLE GAZPACHO

SERVES 4 • PREPARATION: 25 MINUTES • COOKING: 15 MINUTES

6–8 tomatoes
1 cucumber
2 red peppers
1 red onion
1 very small melon or ¼ watermelon
1 avocado
3 tablespoons olive oil
6 slices country-style bread
1–3 small garlic cloves, according to taste, finely chopped
salt and freshly ground pepper
Tabasco sauce

1

Skin the tomatoes by dropping them for 1–2 minutes into boiling water; the skins then slip off easily. Cut each one in half and remove the seeds. Peel and deseed the cucumber and deseed the peppers. Peel and chop the onion. Cut the melon or watermelon, removing all seeds and the skins.

Cut the following into tiny dice: 1 tomato, quarter of the cucumber, 1 slice of melon, 1 avocado, quarter of the onion and quarter of the pepper. Reserve as garnish. Cut the remainder of the vegetables and the melon into large pieces.

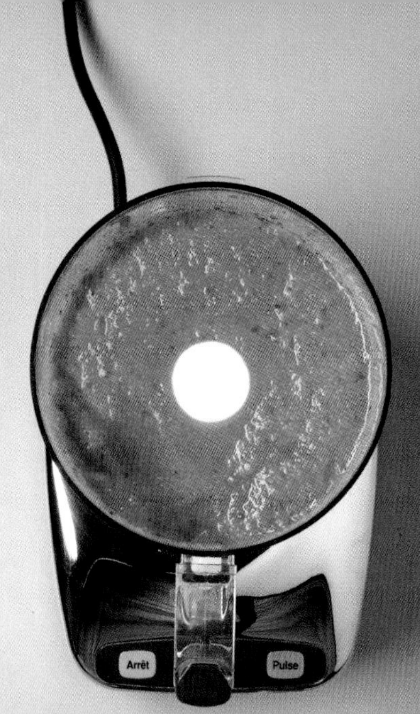

2 3
4 5

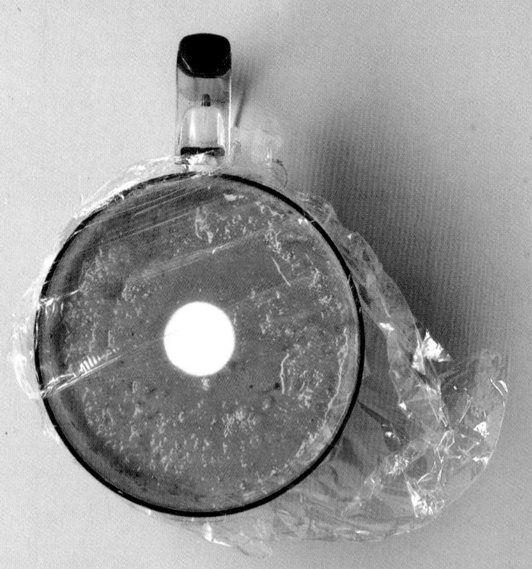

2	Put the roughly chopped vegetables and melon into a food-processor with 2 tablespoons olive oil and 2 slices of bread, crusts removed.	3	Whizz everything until smooth. Season to taste with salt, pepper and Tabasco sauce.
4	Cover with cling film and leave in a cool place for several hours.	5	For the croûtons: preheat the oven to 200°C (400°F), Gas Mark 6. Cut the bread into cubes, spread on a baking sheet, scatter over the garlic and drizzle with oil. Cook for 10–15 minutes.

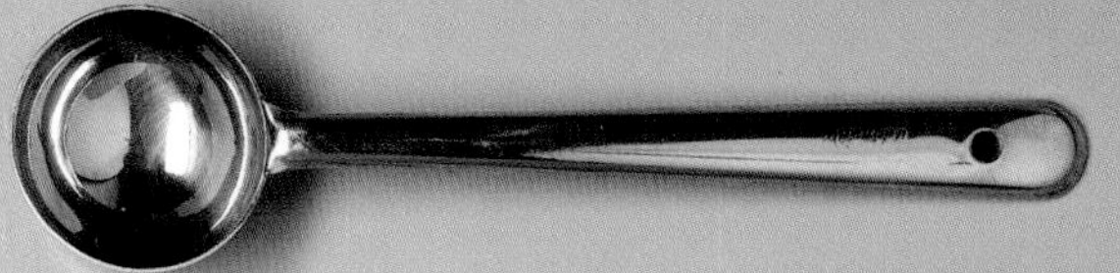

6	Serve the soup well chilled with ice cubes and the reserved vegetables in each bowl. Hand round the croûtons separately.	**OTHER FRUIT IDEAS** Use ripe mango in place of the melon.

TIP	**VARIATION**
☛ The gazpacho is best if it can be chilled for several hours in the fridge before serving.	You can add a large glass of cultured buttermilk if you wish.

SPRING MINESTRONE

SERVES 6 • PREPARATION: 35 MINUTES • COOKING: 3 HOURS 30 MINUTES • SOAKING: OVERNIGHT

100 g (3½ oz) haricot beans (dried or tinned)
3 potatoes
1 fennel bulb
2 small courgettes
¼ spring cabbage

1 onion + 2 garlic cloves
4–6 tablespoons olive oil
250 g (8 oz) cherry tomatoes
3 chicken or vegetable stock cubes, dissolved in 1.5 litres (2½ pints) water

50 g (2 oz) Parmesan + 1 rind of Parmesan
leaves from 4 basil stalks, torn into pieces
salt and freshly ground pepper
100 g (3½ oz) short pasta

1	If using dried haricot beans, put them in cold water to soak overnight.	2	The next day, put the beans in a saucepan with fresh water and cook, uncovered, for 30–40 minutes.	3	Dice the potatoes, fennel and courgettes, and slice the cabbage. Finely chop the onion and garlic.	
4	Heat the oil in a pan. Cook the onion and garlic, then the potatoes, for 2–3 minutes.	5	Add the fennel and cabbage next, and cook for a further 2–3 minutes.	6	Add three-quarters of the tomatoes and the courgettes.	➢

7 8

9 10

7	Pour in the stock then add in the rind of Parmesan and the torn basil leaves. Bring to the boil then reduce the heat to low.	8	Leave to cook for 2 hours, covered, stirring occasionally to prevent it sticking.
9	Taste and adjust the seasoning if necessary. Add the pasta and the reserved courgettes and tomatoes.	10	Add the cooked beans (or the tinned ones, if using) and continue to cook for a further 20 minutes.

11	Serve with Parmesan shavings, pesto and good-quality bread.

RUSTIC FLAVOUR

Minestrone is even better if you add a ham bone with the stock in step 7.

OTHER IDEAS FOR SPRING MINESTRONE

Use broad beans, peas or green beans.

TIP

Minestrone is a meal in itself. Follow it with just a light dessert: a citrus fruit salad or strawberries in season.

56

RED LENTIL DAHL

SERVES 4 • PREPARATION: 15 MINUTES • COOKING: 25 MINUTES

250 g (8 oz) split red lentils
1 onion
1 small tin of tomatoes

$\frac{1}{4}$ teaspoon cumin seeds
1 cinnamon stick
6 green cardamom pods

couple of pinches of turmeric
100 ml ($3\frac{1}{2}$ fl oz) coconut milk
1 lime

1	Rinse the lentils thoroughly in a colander.	2	Put the lentils in a large saucepan with the roughly chopped onion, the tomatoes and the spices.	
3	Add 500 ml (17 fl oz) water. Bring to the boil and cook, uncovered, for about 25 minutes until the lentils start to lose their shape.	4	Remove and discard the cinnamon stick and the cardamom pods.	➢

5 Blend the lentils in a food-processor until smooth.

FOR A MORE PRONOUNCED FLAVOUR

Return the seeds from 1–2 cardamom pods to the lentils just before blending.

IF YOU DON'T HAVE A FOOD-PROCESSOR

You can serve the dahl unblended, in which case you need to chop the onion and the tomatoes finely before adding them to the pan.

6	Return the dahl to the pan over a gentle heat, then add in the coconut milk and a squeeze of lime juice. Serve at once.

OPTION

Instead of the coconut milk you can use Greek-style yogurt.

VARIATIONS

You can make this into a soup by using twice the amount of water for cooking the lentils. Alternatively, you can use less water to cook the lentils then dry them out further in a frying pan with a little oil and ½ teaspoon of garam masala. Serve as a dip.

MASHED POTATO

SERVES 4 • PREPARATION: 20 MINUTES • COOKING: 30 MINUTES

1 kg (2 lb) floury potatoes
salt
50 g (2 oz) butter
3 tablespoons crème fraîche
100 ml (3½ fl oz) milk

IN ADVANCE:
Wash the potatoes.

ESSENTIAL:
Do not be tempted to use a food-processor, the resultant mash will be far too elastic.

1	Put the potatoes in a large saucepan. Cover with cold water, add a little salt and bring to the boil.	2	Allow the potatoes to boil gently with the pan half-covered, for 20–30 minutes, depending on their size.	3	Drain then peel the potatoes. Return them to the pan and allow to dry for a few seconds over the heat.
4	Add the butter and crème fraîche and mash them in using a potato masher.	5	Heat the milk and then beat into the mash using a wooden spoon.	6	Check the seasoning, add salt if necessary and serve immediately.

OVEN-BAKED RATATOUILLE

SERVES 6 • PREPARATION: 25 MINUTES • COOKING: 40 MINUTES

3 large or 6 smaller tomatoes
3 courgettes
2 small aubergines
1–2 red or yellow peppers
1–2 red onions + 1 garlic clove

2 tablespoons olive oil
salt and freshly ground pepper
1 teaspoon vinegar
½ teaspoon sugar
2 basil stalks

IN ADVANCE:
Preheat the oven to 200°C (400°F), Gas Mark 6.

1 2

3 4

1	Wash all the vegetables then cut them into small cubes.	2	Put everything in a shallow-sided baking dish or on a baking tray. Pour in the oil and mix in carefully. Season with salt and pepper.
3	Transfer to the oven and cook for 40 minutes.	4	Add the vinegar mixed with the sugar and sprinkle with chopped basil. Serve hot or cold.

ROASTED ROOT VEGETABLES

SERVES 6 • PREPARATION: 25 MINUTES • COOKING: 1 HOUR

1.5 kg (3 lb) mixed root vegetables: carrots, potatoes, parsnips, Jerusalem artichokes, turnips, celeriac, swede…
3 tablespoons olive oil
4 thyme stalks
4 chervil stalks
4 tablespoons mascarpone
salt and freshly ground pepper

IN ADVANCE:
Preheat the oven to 190°C (375°F), Gas Mark 5.

1 2

3 4

1	Wash and peel all the vegetables and cut them uniformly into large chips.	2	Spread them out on a baking tray, drizzle with oil, tuck in the thyme and mix well.
3	Transfer to the oven and roast for 1 hour.	4	Chop the chervil and mix with the mascarpone, season with salt and pepper and serve over the hot roasted vegetables.

60

STUFFED VEGETABLES

SERVES 4 • PREPARATION: 30 MINUTES • COOKING: 1 HOUR 20 MINUTES

4 medium tomatoes
3 courgettes
2 red peppers
3 onions
3 tablespoons olive oil
3–4 spring onions

1–2 garlic cloves
6 basil sprigs
100 g (3½ oz) minced veal
40 g (1½ oz) Parmesan
1 egg
2 tablespoons breadcrumbs

salt and pepper

IN ADVANCE:
Preheat the oven to 200°C (400°F), Gas Mark 6.

1 2

3 4

1	Wash all the vegetables. Slice the tops off the tomatoes and use a teaspoon to remove the seeds, juice and centres. Reserve.	2	Split the courgettes down their length, remove the seeds and core, keeping about 3–5 mm (¼ in) of flesh on all sides. Reserve.	
3	Cut 1 pepper lengthways and remove the seeds and membranes.	4	Core the onions and reserve the centres.	➢

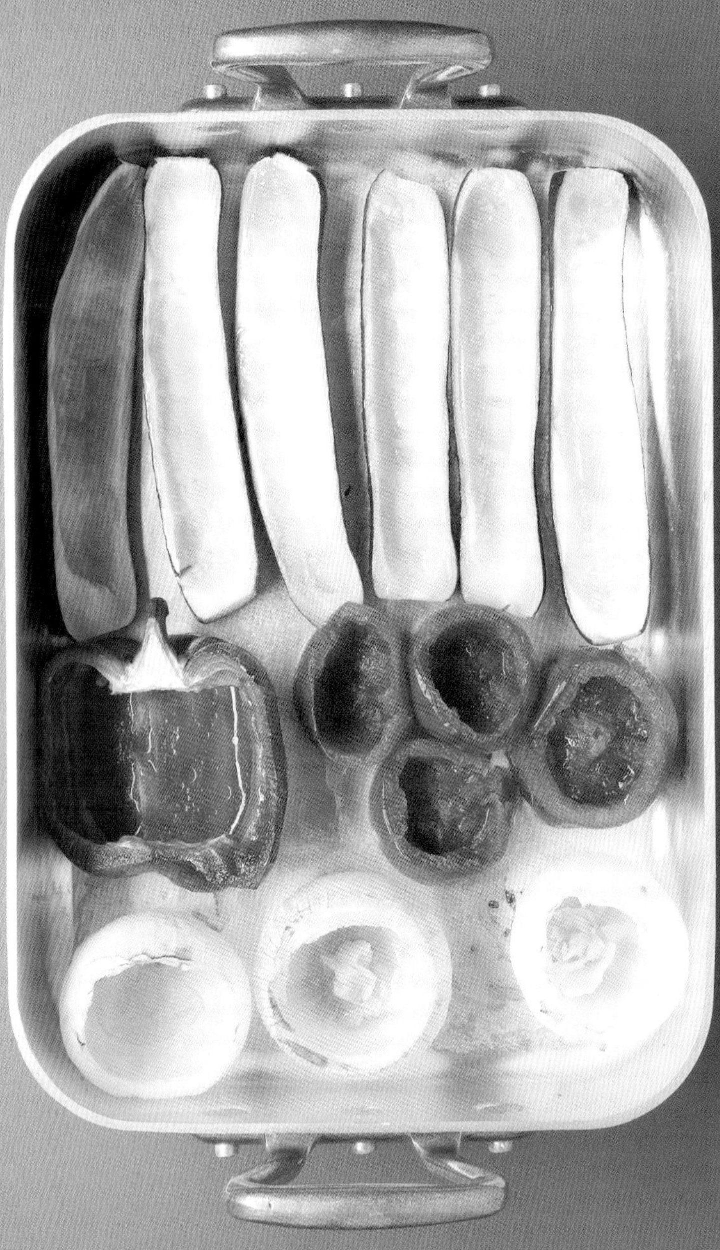

<table>
<tr><td>5</td><td>Put all the prepared vegetables in a baking tray and drizzle with 1 tablespoon of the oil. Transfer to the oven and cook for 20 minutes.</td><td>TIP
☛ Use a pastry brush to make the task of oiling the cored vegetables easier.</td></tr>
<tr><td colspan="2">OPTION
If you can find them, use round courgettes; they are practical to stuff and look attractive.</td><td>TIP
You may wish to cook the onion and pepper for a further 15–20 minutes: they will be softer and less crunchy.</td></tr>
</table>

6 7
8 9

FOR THE STUFFING

6	Chop the reserved vegetable flesh using a food-processor or by hand.	7	Finely chop the spring onions, the remaining pepper, the garlic and basil.
8	Heat the remaining oil in a frying pan and cook the onions for 5 minutes. Add the pepper and cook for a further 5 minutes.	9	Add the chopped vegetables to the pan. Cook, stirring, for 5 minutes. ➢

10 Add the meat to the pan and cook until it is lightly browned. Add the grated Parmesan and the egg. Sprinkle in the breadcrumbs and season with salt and pepper.

OPTION

Veal makes a light stuffing but you can just as well use sausagemeat or minced lamb.

VEGETARIAN STUFFING

Instead of using meat, use the chopped flesh of an extra 2 tomatoes, 2 courgettes and 2 peppers and add in a handful of different chopped herbs to give the dish even more flavour.

11	Fill the prepared vegetables with the stuffing and transfer to the oven for 45 minutes.

SERVING SUGGESTION

Serve with Camargue or risotto rice.

SOFT CHEESE STUFFING

Mix 400 g (13 oz) ricotta, soft sheep's cheese or cottage cheese, ¼ teaspoon harissa paste and ½ bunch of chopped flat leaf parsley. Stuff the prepared vegetables as before and cook in the oven for a further 20 minutes.

61

COURGETTE CRUMBLE

SERVES 4 • PREPARATION: 25 MINUTES • COOKING: 45 MINUTES

4 tablespoons whole almonds
1 kg (2 lb) courgettes, washed and trimmed
salt and freshly ground pepper
2 tablespoons olive oil
75 g (3 oz) butter

150 g (5 oz) wholemeal flour
¼ teaspoon sugar
¼ teaspoon vinegar
200 g (7 oz) cottage cheese
leaves from 6 basil stalks, chopped

IN ADVANCE:
Preheat the oven to 220°C (425°F), Gas Mark 7. Roughly chop the almonds.

1	Coarsely grate the courgettes. Season with salt and pepper and drizzle with 1 tablespoon of olive oil.	2	Transfer to a gratin dish and cook at the top of the oven for 15 minutes.	3	Use your fingertips to rub the butter into the flour. Add the remaining oil and the almonds. Season with salt.
4	Mix the sugar and vinegar with the courgettes, then the cottage cheese and basil.	5	Spread the crumble over the dish. Set the oven to 180°C (350°F), Gas Mark 4.	6	Transfer to the oven and bake the crumble for 25 minutes to brown the top.

CREAMY POTATO GRATIN

⇝ SERVES 6 • PREPARATION: 20 MINUTES • COOKING: 1 HOUR 30 MINUTES ⇜

1 kg (2 lb) waxy potatoes (such as Charlotte or Desirée)
1 garlic clove
25 g (1 oz) butter

salt and freshly ground pepper
600 ml (1 pint) double cream

IN ADVANCE:
Preheat the oven to 160°C (325°F), Gas Mark 3.

62

1 2

3 4

1	Peel the potatoes and cut into very thin slices (3 mm/⅛ in), either by hand or using a food-processor.	2	Cut the garlic clove in half and rub them over the sides and base of a large gratin dish. Butter the dish generously.
3	Put the sliced potatoes in the dish and season with salt and pepper. Pour over the cream to cover.	4	Transfer to the oven for 1¼–1½ hours, by which time the top should be crisp and golden, the potatoes cooked and the cream reduced.

63

FRENCH PIZZA (PISSALADIÈRE)

SERVES 4 • PREPARATION: 15 MINUTES • COOKING: 1 HOUR

10 onions
3 tablespoons oil or 40 g (1½ oz) butter
200 g (7 oz) good-quality ready-rolled puff pastry (preferably all-butter)
½ teaspoon dried oregano
4–8 anchovies in oil (optional)

IN ADVANCE:
Preheat the oven to 220°C (425°F), Gas Mark 7. Cut the anchovies (if using) into thin fillets.

1 2

3 4

1	Peel and halve the onions then cut them into slices, not too thinly.	2	Heat the oil or butter in a pan with the onions. Leave them to soften for 30–35 minutes over a very gentle heat.
3	Unroll the pastry on to a baking sheet and prick with a fork. Mark a 1-cm (½-in) border. Spread the cooked onions up to the border and sprinkle with oregano. Top with anchovies.	4	Cook in the oven for about 20 minutes or until the pastry is golden brown. Serve with a green salad.

VEGETABLE HOT-POT

SERVES 6 • PREPARATION: 20 MINUTES • COOKING: 15 MINUTES

8 small young carrots or 4 large ones
8 small young turnips or 4–5 medium ones
10 radishes
8 chive or spring onions
2 apples
2 small pears
1 lemon
1–2 tablespoons olive oil
1 small bunch of grapes
salt and freshly ground pepper
1 glass of cider
2 handfuls of baby spinach leaves

1 2

3 4

1	Wash the vegetables and scrape or peel them only if necessary.	2	Cut them into roughly even-sized pieces if they are large. Peel the apples and pears, cut them into quarters and rub with lemon juice.	
3	Heat the oil in a heavy-based, lidded casserole over a medium-high heat. Add in all the vegetables and stir for 3 minutes.	4	Add the fruits, reserving ½ an apple and ½ a pear. Allow everything to colour, stirring, for 2–3 minutes. Season.	➢

5 6

7 8

5	Pour in the cider.	6	Cover the casserole, reduce the heat to low and cook for no more than 10 minutes.
7	Stir in the spinach leaves.	8	Grate the reserved apple and pear.

9	Add the grated apple and pear to the dish. It is delicious served with brown rice and a drizzle of olive oil.

TIP

☛ Rubbing the quartered apples and pears with lemon juice prevents them from discolouring.

VARIATION

Use rocket leaves in place of spinach for a more peppery flavour.

65

VEGETABLE COUSCOUS

SERVES 6 • PREPARATION: 25 MINUTES • COOKING: 45 MINUTES

3–4 carrots, 3–4 turnips, 3 courgettes
1 slice of pumpkin or butternut squash
2–3 potatoes
2 large onions + 2 garlic cloves
1 orange
3 tablespoons olive oil

½ teaspoon ras-el-hanout
1 litre (1¾ pints) vegetable stock (2–3 cubes)
400 g (14 oz) good-quality tinned tomatoes
1 cinnamon stick
1 pinch of saffron threads
275 g (9 oz) tinned chick peas

6 tablespoons sultanas
500 g (1lb) medium couscous
25 g (1 oz) butter
6 tablespoons pine nuts
harissa
½ bunch of flat leaf parsley

1 2

3 4

1	Wash, peel and cut the vegetables into large pieces. Finely chop the garlic and grate the rind of the orange.	2	Heat the oil in a stockpot over a medium heat. Add the onion and cook, stirring, for 5 minutes then add the garlic and cook for 1 minute. Add the ras-el-hanout and stir for a further minute.	
3	Tip in all the prepared vegetables and stir for 5 minutes.	4	Pour in the stock and the tinned tomatoes. Bring to the boil.	➢

5 Put in the cinnamon stick and the saffron, the orange rind, the drained chick peas and the sultanas. Leave to cook for 30 minutes.

QUICK VERSION

You can buy precooked couscous, in which case, simply follow the instructions on the packet to prepare it.

THE ADVANTAGE OF A COUSCOUS STEAMER

With this appliance, the meat and vegetables cook underneath, creating a flavoured stock that steams the couscous in the basket on top. If the holes in the basket are large, put in a piece of muslin cloth before tipping in the couscous. If you don't have a couscous steamer, use a large stockpot and put a steaming basket on top.

6	Prepare the couscous while the vegetables cook: cover the grains with cold water in a bowl and leave to soak for 10 minutes.	7	Separate the grains using your hands then put the couscous in a steaming basket that will sit on top of the vegetables. Dot little pieces of butter over the top of the couscous.
8	Steam for about 20 minutes, covered with a lid, on top of the vegetables if possible.	9	Serve the vegetables with the stock and the couscous sprinkled with pine nuts (dry roasted in a pan for more flavour) with piquant harissa.

HERBY BULGAR WHEAT SALAD

SERVES 4 • PREPARATION: 25 MINUTES • RESTING: 15 MINUTES

2 good bunches of flat leaf parsley
1 good bunch of mint
75 g (3 oz) bulgar wheat
2 small cucumbers
1 small red onion
2 tablespoons almonds, skinned and lightly toasted in a frying pan
6–8 tablespoons lemon juice (1–2 lemons)
salt and freshly ground pepper
2 tablespoons olive oil or a little more as necessary

1 2

3 4

1	Wash and drain the herbs then strip off the leaves.	2	Chop them finely by hand. (You can also chop them in a food processor but only briefly, so that they are not chopped too finely.)	
3	Cover the bulgar wheat with cold water and leave to soak for 15 minutes. (Some bulgar wheat needs to be cooked: do check the instructions on the packet.)	4	Peel the cucumbers, cut in half lengthways and remove the seeds. Cut the halves into small dice. Finely chop the onion.	➢

5	Drain the bulgar wheat and combine all the ingredients in a large salad bowl.	**VARIATION** You can of course add 2–3 tomatoes, peeled, deseeded and cut into small dice.

6 To season: first add the lemon juice. Taste and adjust with salt, pepper, olive oil and extra lemon juice as required.

SERVING IDEAS

This salad is excellent for a picnic or to serve with a barbecue.

OTHER INGREDIENTS

You can also use large- or medium-grain couscous. But bulgar or cracked wheat has a nutty flavour and a more interesting texture. You need to use mild onions or try with 4–5 spring onions.

STIR-FRIED VEGETABLES

SERVES 1 • PREPARATION: 15 MINUTES • COOKING: 3 MINUTES

3 Swiss chard, including all leaves
1 handful shiitaké, wild or cultivated mushrooms
1 garlic clove
1 small knob of ginger

3 spring onions
2 tablespoons vegetable oil
1 tablespoon oyster or soy sauce
½ teaspoon cornflour

IN ADVANCE:
Preheat the oven to 220°C (425°F), Gas Mark 7. Wash the chard.

1	Separate the white stalks from the chard leaves. Finely chop everything. Wipe the mushrooms and cut into thin slices. Finely chop the garlic and the peeled ginger. Chop the spring onions.	2	Heat a wok over the highest heat until hot and smoking. Pour in the oil. Throw in the onions, garlic and ginger and stir-fry rapidly for 30 seconds.
3	Add the chard stalks and the mushrooms and stir-fry, stirring constantly, for 2 minutes. Add the chard leaves and cook for a further minute.	4	Mix the oyster or soy sauce with the cornflour and stir into the wok. Leave to cook for 1 minute then serve.

JAPANESE TEMPURA

✣ **SERVES 4** • PREPARATION: 20 MINUTES • COOKING: 2 MINUTES ✣

250 ml (8 fl oz) iced water
225 g (8 oz) flour
¼ teaspoon baking powder
oil, for deep frying
salt flakes

selection of vegetables: young celery leaves, cultivated or wild mushrooms, spring onions, sliced sweet potato or pumpkin, courgette flowers, and so forth

IN ADVANCE:
Finely slice all the vegetables and above all ensure they are completely dry. Heat the oil in a deep fryer to 190°C (375°F).

1	Put the iced water in a salad bowl. Add the flour and the baking powder.	2	Mix together lightly; there should still be some lumps remaining in the batter.	3	When the oil is hot, dip the prepared vegetables in the batter.
4	Drop the coated vegetables in the hot oil. Don't try to cook too many at a time.	5	Turn over the slices after just a few seconds and remove before they brown.	6	Drain on kitchen paper. Serve immediately with the salt flakes.

DESSERTS

CREAMY

TEATIME

CAKES

FRUITY

EASY RICE PUDDING

SERVES 4 • PREPARATION: 5 MINUTES • COOKING: 35 MINUTES

150 g (5 oz) round grain rice
750 ml (1¼ pints) milk
200 ml (7 fl oz) crème fraîche
1 vanilla pod
1 tablespoon sugar
15 g (½ oz) butter

VARIATION:
Stir in 1 teaspoon rose water + 1 extra tablespoon sugar at the end.

1 2
3 4

1	Put the rice, milk, crème fraîche and the vanilla pod in a large saucepan. Add a glass of water and bring to the boil.	2	Lower the heat and cook, uncovered, gently bubbling, for 35 minutes, by which time the rice should be creamy but still slightly al dente.
3	Add the sugar and the butter.	4	Serve hot or cold.

RHUBARB CRÈME BRÛLÉE

SERVES 4 • PREPARATION: 25 MINUTES • COOKING: 1 HOUR • RESTING: 1 HOUR

300 g (10 oz) frozen rhubarb
200 g (7 oz) sugar
300 ml (½ pint) double cream

200 ml (7 fl oz) milk
1 vanilla pod
8 egg yolks

IN ADVANCE:
Preheat the oven to 180°C (350°F), Gas Mark 4.

1 2
3 4

1	Put the rhubarb in an ovenproof dish with 3 tablespoons of the sugar.	2	Transfer to the oven and cook for 30 minutes. Reduce the temperature to 140°C (275°F), Gas Mark 1.	
3	Pour the cream and the milk into a saucepan. Add the vanilla pod split lengthways, scraping the seeds into the cream/milk mixture. Bring gently to the boil.	4	Whisk together the egg yolks with 5 tablespoons of the sugar until the mixture is light and creamy.	➢

5	Whisk in the hot cream/milk a little at a time. Put the ovenproof dish in a larger one filled with hot water to come halfway up the sides.	6	Gently pour the custard over the rhubarb. Transfer the dish and its bain-marie to the oven and cook for 25 minutes.
7	Allow to cool then place in the fridge.	8	When you are ready to serve, preheat the grill to its highest setting and sprinkle the remaining sugar over the chilled custard.

9	Caramelize the sugar under the hot grill and serve immediately.	**VARIATION** In place of ordinary granulated sugar, try using raw cane sugar, which is very good caramelized.

TIP

The custard needs to be very cold before you flash it under the grill to brown the sugar.

EQUIPMENT

An ordinary grill doesn't always give the best brûlée topping – a cook's blowtorch is ideal for caramelizing the sugar.

71

ITALIAN-STYLE TRIFLE

SERVES 4 • PREPARATION: 30 MINUTES • COOKING: 15 MINUTES • RESTING: OVERNIGHT

350 ml (12 fl oz) milk
1 vanilla pod
3 egg yolks
5 tablespoons sugar

2–3 slices of pandoro or panettone
3–4 amaretti (Italian macaroons)
4–5 slices of plain cake

1 glass of muscat and a dash of Grand Marnier (or other orange liqueur)
1 large punnet (500 g/1 lb) raspberries
300 ml (½ pint) whipping cream

1 2
3 4

1	First make the custard: gently heat the milk with the vanilla pod, split lengthways, in a small casserole.	2	In a second, larger pan, whisk the egg yolks with 4 tablespoons of the sugar.	
3	Pour the near-boiling milk over the egg mixture and whisk.	4	Place the pan over a gentle heat and stir constantly until the custard thickens. Set aside and allow to cool.	➢

5	Line the base of a shallow-sided glass bowl with the cake slices. Sprinkle with the muscat and Grand Marnier.	6	Reserving a few to decorate, crush the raspberries with the remaining sugar and spread over the cake.	7	Whip the cream until soft peaks form.
8	Mix one-third of the whipped cream with the cold custard.	9	Spread this mixture over the raspberries.	10	Top with the rest of the whipped cream.

		CHILD-FRIENDLY VERSION
11	Place in the fridge until the following day. When you are ready to serve, decorate with the reserved whole raspberries.	Use orange juice instead of the alcohol.

DECORATION

A few flaked almonds or crystallized violets make an attractive alternative decoration.

VARIATIONS

This is a classic trifle recipe but it also works very well with strawberres and a few slices of banana – dip them in lemon juice to prevent any discolouration.

FLOATING ISLANDS

SERVES 3 • PREPARATION: 15 MINUTES • COOKING: 20 MINUTES

Custard (see recipe 71)
3 egg whites
1 pinch of salt

3 tablespoons sugar
1 litre (1¾ pints) milk

CARAMEL:
2 tablespoons water
3 tablespoons sugar

1	First make the custard (follow recipe 71 for the method).	2	Divide between 3 small bowls or ramekin dishes and leave to cool before transferring to the fridge.	
3	Put the egg whites in a large bowl with the pinch of salt.	4	Whisk the whites into stiff peaks. Add the sugar and whisk again.	➢

5 6

7 8

5	Heat the milk in a small saucepan. When it starts to simmer, reduce the heat to keep it at simmering point. Drop in spoonfuls of egg white and poach for 2 minutes on each side.	6	Remove the poached whites to drain on kitchen paper then place them on top of the custard in the bowls.
7	Make the caramel: put the water and the sugar in a small pan and heat.	8	As soon as it takes on a golden colour, pour it over the floating islands.

9	Serve immediately.	**OPTIONS** Flavour the milk for the custard as it heats with 2–3 cardamom pods or 2–3 drops of rose water.

HOW TO POACH THE WHITES

Drop large spoonfuls of the beaten egg white into the hot milk. After 2 minutes turn them over and leave to cook for a further 2 minutes.

VARIATIONS

In place of the caramel, decorate the islands with chocolate shavings or crushed praline.

PANCAKES

→ **SERVES 4** • PREPARATION: 15 MINUTES • COOKING: 30 MINUTES ←

125 g (4 oz) sifted flour
pinch of salt
4 eggs

400 ml (14 fl oz) milk
butter, for greasing
unsalted butter (optional)

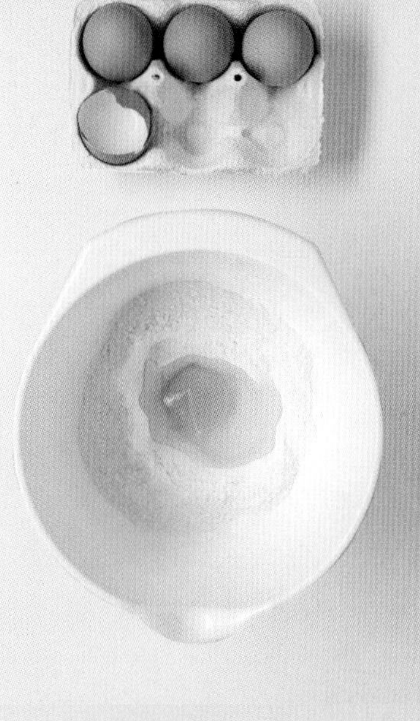

1 2
3 4

1	Put the flour in a large mixing bowl with the pinch of salt. Make a well in the centre and break 1 egg into the middle.	2	Mix with a wooden spoon to incorporate the flour into the egg, a little at a time. Do the same with the 3 remaining eggs.	
3	Little by little add the milk, beating to incorporate well.	4	Cover the batter with cling film and allow to rest in the fridge for at least 1 hour.	➢

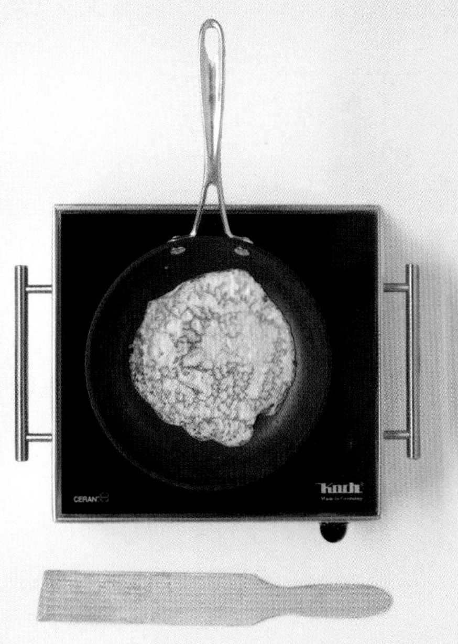

5	Heat a 20-cm (8-in) nonstick frying pan over a high heat. Grease the pan generously with a knob of butter on a sheet of kitchen paper.	6	Reduce the heat to medium. Pour in a small ladleful of batter.
7	The first side is cooked when the pancake becomes detached from the base of the frying pan; this takes about 1 minute.	8	Flip the pancake with a quick shake of the pan, or use a wooden spatula. The second side cooks in about 30 seconds.

9	Slide out the cooked pancake onto a plate and spread a little unsalted butter over it if you wish. Grease the pan again with the buttered kitchen paper before cooking the next pancake. Continue in this way until all the batter is used up.	**TO SERVE** Serve with lemon or orange juice and sugar, or with honey, jam, chocolate spread, sweetened chestnut purée, and so forth. **PANCAKE CAKE** Layer the pancakes in a large pile with a drizzle of lightly sweetened orange juice between the layers.

EGGY BREAD

SERVES 2 • PREPARATION: 10 MINUTES • COOKING: 6 MINUTES

1 egg
1 glass of milk
1 tablespoon sugar
4 slices of stale brioche or soft-batch bread
2 tablespoons butter
1 teaspoon ground cinnamon

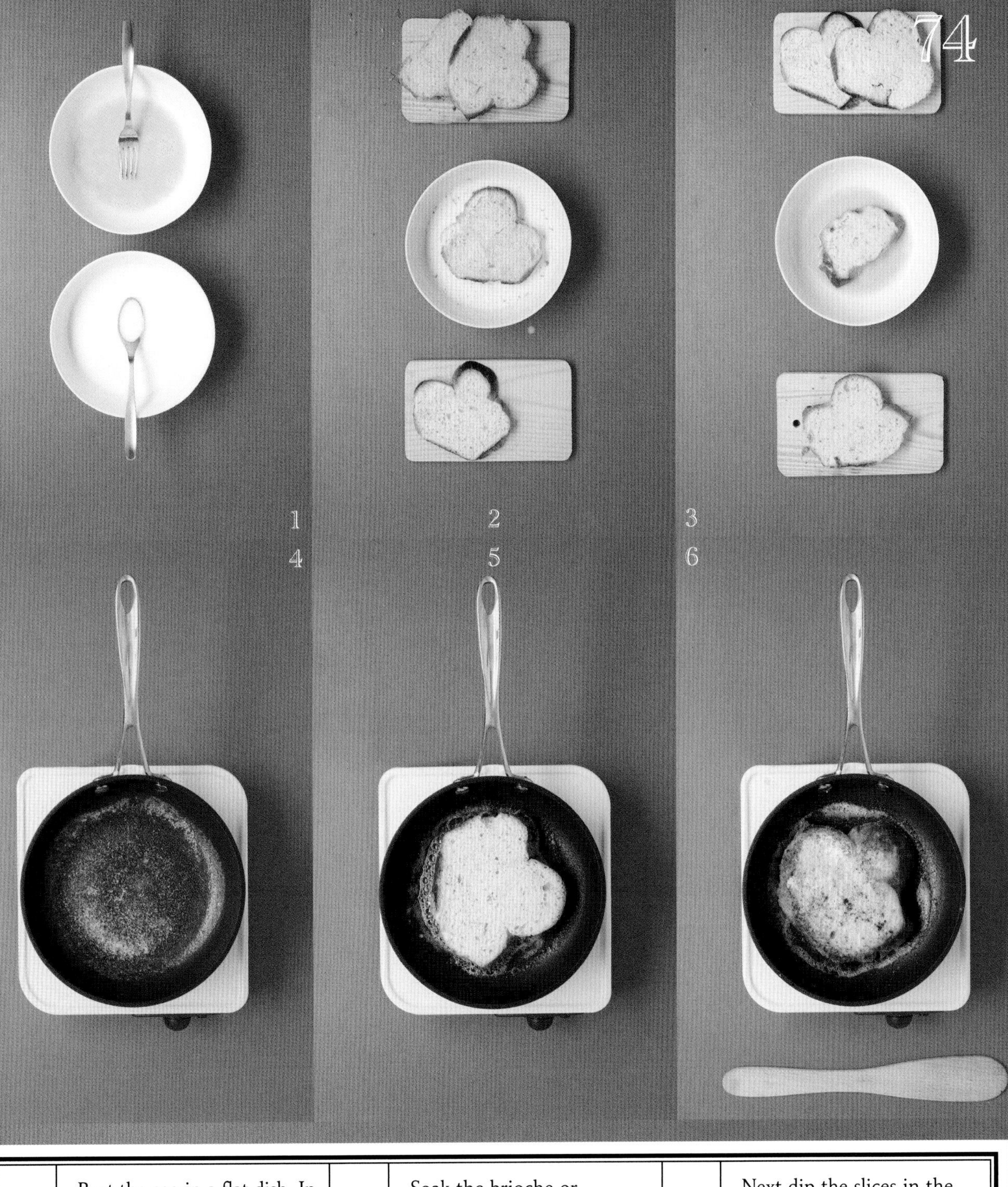

1	Beat the egg in a flat dish. In a second dish mix the milk with ½ teaspoon of sugar.	2	Soak the brioche or bread slices in the sweetened milk.	3	Next dip the slices in the beaten egg.
4	Melt the butter in a frying pan over a medium heat.	5	Fry the dipped slices, one at a time, in the hot butter for about 3 minutes on one side.	6	Flip over the slices, cook for a further 3 minutes, sprinkle with sugar and cinnamon and serve immediately.

CHEESECAKE

SERVES 6 • PREPARATION: 30 MINUTES • COOKING: 55 MINUTES • RESTING: 1–2 DAYS

150 g (5 oz) plain biscuits or digestives
50 g (2 oz) butter
50 g (2 oz) desiccated coconut
750 g (1½ lb) cream cheese
150 g (5 oz) sugar

2 tablespoons flour
rind and juice of 2 limes and 1 lemon
4 eggs
125 g (4 oz) crème fraîche
1 vanilla pod

IN ADVANCE:
Preheat the oven to 180°C (350°F), Gas Mark 4.

1	Put the biscuits into a large plastic bag, tie loosely and crush with a rolling pin until they form crumbs.	2	Melt the butter in a small saucepan, remove from the heat, and mix in the biscuit crumbs and desiccated coconut.	
3	Press this mixture into a 28-cm (11-in) springform cake tin. Transfer to the oven and cook for 10 minutes.	4	Remove from the oven and reduce the temperature to 140°C (275°F), Gas Mark 1.	➢

5	Beat the cream cheese briefly, just until it is smooth, either in a food-processor or by whisking in a large bowl. Incorporate the sugar, then the flour and the citrus rind and juices.	6	Stir in the eggs, one by one.
7	Add the crème fraîche.	8	Pour into the cake tin and transfer to the oven for 45 minutes to 1 hour, by which time the sides should be set but the centre still wobbly.

9	Switch off the oven and leave the cheesecake inside for 1 hour then remove and allow to cool. Remove from the tin and refrigerate overnight.

SERVING SUGGESTIONS

Serve the cheesecake with a little raspberry coulis or lemon curd.

OPTION

☛ The cheesecake is at its best served one or even two days after it is made.

VARIATION

For a lighter texture, separate the eggs, add the yolks in step 6 and whisk the whites until firm and fold in after the crème fraîche in step 7.

PRUNE CLAFOUTIS

SERVES 4 • PREPARATION: 10 MINUTES • COOKING: 40 MINUTES

375 g (12 oz) pitted prunes
1 tablespoon rum
4 eggs
75 g (3 oz) flour
50 g (2 oz) sugar + 1 extra tablespoon

200 ml (7 fl oz) crème fraîche (or single cream for a lighter version)
200 ml (7 fl oz) milk
pinch of salt
25 g (1 oz) salted butter

IN ADVANCE:
Soak the prunes in the rum. Preheat the oven to 200°C (400°F),Gas Mark 6.

76

1 2

3 4

1	In a large bowl, whisk together all the ingredients except for the rum and the prunes.	2	Butter a medium-size ovenproof dish. Put the prunes, with the rum, in the dish and pour the whisked mixture on top.
3	Transfer to the oven and cook for 40 minutes: the custard should be set and the surface risen and golden brown.	4	As it cools the custard will deflate. Sprinkle the surface with the tablespoon of sugar and serve warm or cold.

RASPBERRY CLAFOUTIS

VARIATION ON PRUNE CLAFOUTIS

☛ Replace the prunes in recipe 76 with 2 punnets of raspberries, and flavour with a few drops of vanilla extract or the seeds scraped from a vanilla pod instead of the rum.

APRICOT CLAFOUTIS

VARIATION ON PRUNE CLAFOUTIS

☛ Replace the prunes in recipe 76 with 250 g (8 oz) pitted apricots, and flavour with a few drops of vanilla extract or the seeds scraped from a vanilla pod instead of the rum. Sprinkle with flaked almonds.

BAKED APPLES

SERVES 4 • PREPARATION: 10 MINUTES • COOKING: 40 MINUTES

8–12 eating apples, preferably Russets
1 vanilla pod
40 g (1½ oz) salted butter

IN ADVANCE:
Preheat the oven to 190°C (375°F), Gas Mark 5.

1 2

3 4

1	Wash and core the apples with a small pointed knife or a corer. Place them in a baking tin.	2	Split the vanilla pod lengthways then cut into pieces. Poke one piece into the core of each apple with a small knob of butter.
3	Transfer to the oven and cook for about 40 minutes. Serve the baked apples just as they are, with a little crème fraîche or fromage blanc.	4	**TO MAKE COMPÔTE** Scoop out the flesh from the skins with a spoon. Scrape the vanilla seeds from the pod and mix the seeds into the compôte with a fork.

APPLE & PEAR CRUMBLE

SERVES 4 • PREPARATION: 15 MINUTES • COOKING: 35 MINUTES

150 g (5 oz) flour
125 g (4 oz) butter
1–2 tablespoons sugar
compôte (see recipe 79)
3 pears

4 tablespoons lemon juice
1 vanilla pod (optional)
2 tablespoons flaked almonds
crème fraîche to serve

IN ADVANCE:
Preheat the oven to 190°C (375°F), Gas Mark 5.

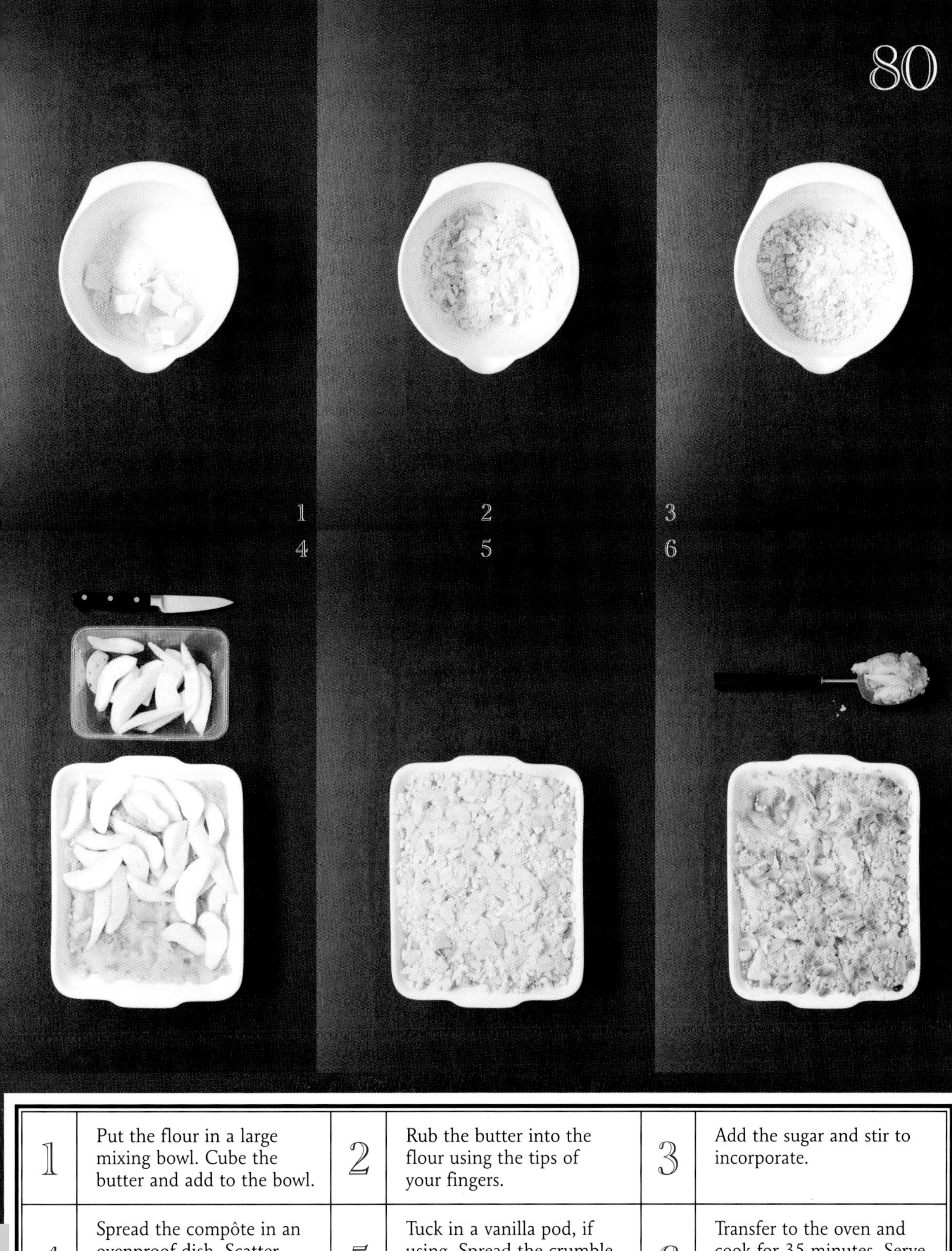

1	Put the flour in a large mixing bowl. Cube the butter and add to the bowl.	2	Rub the butter into the flour using the tips of your fingers.	3	Add the sugar and stir to incorporate.
4	Spread the compôte in an ovenproof dish. Scatter with slices of pear and sprinkle with lemon juice.	5	Tuck in a vanilla pod, if using. Spread the crumble mixture over the fruit and scatter with almonds.	6	Transfer to the oven and cook for 35 minutes. Serve with crème fraîche.

BALSAMIC STRAWBERRIES

SERVES 4 • PREPARATION: 10 MINUTES • RESTING: MINIMUM 30 MINUTES

2 punnets of strawberries
3 tablespoons sugar
3 tablespoons balsamic vinegar

1 2
3 4

1	Wash and hull the strawberries.	2	Mix together the sugar and the balsamic vinegar in a large bowl.
3	Cut the strawberries into halves or quarters, depending on size.	4	Put the strawberries in the bowl and gently stir to coat in the balsamic vinegar. Leave to stand for 30 minutes to 1 hour before serving.

PEARS BELLE-HÉLÈNE

SERVES 4 • PREPARATION: 15 MINUTES • COOKING: 20 MINUTES

4–6 perfect pears, not too ripe and quite firm
2 tablespoons sugar

200 g (7 oz) chocolate, milk or plain
2 tablespoons crème fraîche
vanilla ice cream, to serve

IN ADVANCE:
Peel and core the pears but keep them whole.

1	Heat a saucepan of water with the sugar. When it starts to bubble, add the pears and leave them to poach for about 10 minutes, until the point of a knife pierces them easily.	2	Melt the chocolate in a heat-resistant bowl over a pan of barely simmering water, off the heat.
3	When the chocolate has melted, stir in the crème fraîche.	4	Serve the pears with the chocolate sauce and vanilla ice cream.

83

PEAR & CHOCOLATE TART

SERVES 4 • PREPARATION: 20 MINUTES • COOKING: 40 MINUTES

butter, for greasing
3–4 tablespoons sugar
300 g (10 oz) prepared Shortcrust Pastry (see recipe 08)

100 g (3½ oz) chocolate
4 ripe pears
125 ml (4 fl oz) whipping cream
1 egg

IN ADVANCE:
Preheat the oven to 190°C (375°F), Gas Mark 5.

THE RECIPE BY STAGES	OPTION
Butter a 23-cm (9-in) tart tin and sprinkle with 2 tablespoons sugar. Roll out the pastry and line the tin. Roughly chop the chocolate and distribute over the pastry. Peel and finely slice the pears. Arrange in spiral fashion over the chocolate. Mix the cream, egg and 1 tablespoon of sugar and pour over the pears. Transfer to the oven and bake for 30–35 minutes.	Sprinkle the remaining tablespoon of sugar over the cooked tart and flash under a hot grill to caramelize. **NOTES** ☛ If you can't find ripe pears, use tinned ones or, better still, poach some underripe pears (see recipe 82) yourself.

APPENDICES

GLOSSARY

TABLE OF CONTENTS

RECIPE INDEX

GENERAL INDEX

ACKNOWLEDGEMENTS

GLOSSARY

AL DENTE
An Italian term used to describe the still slightly firm texture of rice grains, pasta or green beans when there is still a little 'bite', that is, not too cooked.

BACON, RINDLESS STREAKY
Good-quality rashers should be used in preference to the pre-cubed lardons.

BAIN-MARIE
When you want to cook, melt or simply heat a dish or an ingredient gently, this is easily achieved by placing a heat-resistant bowl over a saucepan of gently simmering water (either over the heat or away from it) or by using a specially designed double saucepan, or by placing the dish inside another, larger one which is half-filled with hot water and placed in the oven. The food is, in effect, cooked in a water bath; the heat is very gentle and there is no risk of the ingredients burning or the dish drying out. A bain-marie is perfect for melting chocolate and equally for emulsifying a mixture that contains egg yolks (such as sabayon, sauces and so forth).

BONES
You can remove the bones from a fillet of fish by pulling them out with your fingertips or, better, with a pair of fish tweezers.

BRAISE
This means to cook meat or vegetables in a tightly lidded casserole or covered dish over a very low heat and in liquid (stock, water, wine, cider...).

BREADCRUMBS
You can buy ready-made breadcrumbs or, better still, make them yourself using stale bread either by whizzing it in a food-processor or crushing it with a rolling pin. You can also make crumbs using fresh bread but the texture is less even and so not good for coating food such as fish fillets.

BROWN
This means to cook ingredients cut into small pieces over a medium heat in fat or oil. They need to be stirred from time to time to ensure they colour evenly on all sides.

BULGAR WHEAT
This is cracked wheat. It has a flavour and texture that is superior to couscous for use in salads.

BUTTER
Salted or unsalted, the choice is yours, even for cakes.

CEVICHE
This fish dish originates from South America and consists of slices of raw fish that is 'cooked' in lemon or lime juice.

CHANTILLY
This is a cream suitable for piping made from whipping very cold liquid or pouring cream. It is easiest made using a hand-held electric whisk but it is possible to whip chantilly with a hand whisk. You can sweeten it and flavour it as you wish (vanilla, Grand Marnier...).

COCONUT MILK
Look for coconut milk sold in cartons, which is creamier and superior to the tinned version which tends to separate. However, if you can only find tinned coconut milk, it's easy enough to stir it to a homogeneous consistency.

CRUMBS
Crumbs are made by rubbing small pieces of butter into flour with your fingertips. The butter must be kept cold and lifting your hands as you work keeps it aerated and therefore cold. You can also make crumbs in a food-processor fitted with a blade. Put the flour and the cold cubed butter into the bowl and pulse for a few seconds. These crumbs form the basis of shortcrust pastry and crumbles.

MOZZARELLA
Opt for buffalo mozzarella where there is a choice – it has far more flavour.

PANCETTA
An Italian cured meat made from pork belly. It is usually sold thinly sliced.

PANDORO
A traditional Italian sweet yeast bread similar in style to panettone but without raisins and candied peel. Like panettone, it is usually found in the shops at Christmas time. Use it like sponge cake to soak up alcohol or fruit juice in desserts such as trifle.

POACH
This refers to dropping an ingredient into gently simmering liquid – water, milk or syrup – to cook it. Poached dishes include fruit such as pears, egg white to make floating islands and poached egg.

REDUCE
You reduce the volume of a liquid by boiling it to evaporate off some of the water content.

RICE
For rice pudding and risotto make sure you use round grain rice (arborio, vialone nano…). For a pilaf, you need long grain, such as basmati, which is prized for its delicate aroma.

ROAST
This is a method of cooking ingredients (meat, fish steaks, vegetables, fruit), either whole or in large pieces, uncovered and without liquid. Roasting is done in the oven, with or without a rotisserie (or over a barbecue). Often the food is basted with a little fat to glaze and colour it and to prevent it drying out.

ROOT VEGETABLES
Don't underestimate the humble root vegetables! Cleaned and peeled, they are easy to cook and have a delicious flavour.

SEAL
This refers to placing an ingredient (usually meat or fish) in contact with the surface of a very hot frying pan to quickly seal and cook it first on one side and then the other.

SAUTÉ
A term to describe a quick cooking method using either a frying pan or a wok over a medium to high heat, usually with a little fat or oil. The ingredients are generally cut into small pieces and moved around by shaking the pan or stirring the food with a wooden spoon or spatula.

SCALE (FISH)
Ask your fishmonger to do this for you.

SIMMER
This means cooking a dish over a very low heat. It will bubble gently.

STOCK
The best stock, of course, is what you make yourself, but when time is short, use good-quality stock cubes or powder. Try to find organic stock cubes, which have the advantage of being free from artificial flavour enhancers. Allow half a stock cube for every ½ litre (17 fl oz) of water.

VANILLA
For preference, always choose a vanilla pod (split it into two lengthways and scrape out the sticky seeds with a small spoon or the tip of a knife) or natural vanilla extract. It is far better than vanilla 'essence'.

WHISKED EGG WHITE
To successfully whisk egg whites, you need to ensure that not the slightest speck of yolk gets into the whites when you separate them and that the bowl and beaters are scrupulously clean and free of any grease. The trick is to whisk the whites fast at the end so that they rise in firm peaks. Incorporate the whisked egg whites gently into a mixture so that the air is not knocked out.

TABLE OF CONTENTS

1

THE CLASSICS

SALADS

BASICS

EGGS

STEAK & CO.

2

PASTA & RICE

SAUCES

PASTA

RICE

3

MEAT

ROASTS

STEWS

WORLD

4

FISH & SHELLFISH

CLASSICS

PAN-FRIED

MARINATED

5

VEGETABLES

SOUPS & CO.

BAKED VEGETABLES

ONE-POT VEGETABLES

RAW & SIMPLY COOKED

6

DESSERTS

CREAMY

TEATIME

CAKES

FRUITY

INDEX OF RECIPES

Note: This index is organized by recipe number.

GENERAL INDEX

Note: This index is organized by recipe number.

ACKNOWLEDGEMENTS

The author and publishers wish to thank Magimix for the loan of their food-processors and deep fryer.
www.magimix.com
Customer service: (+33) 01-43-98-36-36

With thanks to the Lucano family.

Props: Emmanuelle Javelle
Design: Alexandre Nicolas
English translation and adaptation: JMS Books llp
Layout: cbdesign